Brief Cognitive Behaviour Therapy

Brief Therapies Series

Series Editor: Stephen Palmer
Associate Editor: Gladeana McMahon

Focusing on brief and time-limited therapies, this series of books is aimed at students, beginning and experienced counsellors, therapists and other members of the helping professions who need to know more about working with the specific skills, theories and practices involving in this demanding but vital area of their work.

Books in the series:

Solution-Focused Therapy
Bill O'Connell

*A Psychodynamic Approach to Brief
Counselling and Psychotherapy*
Gertrud Mander

Brief Cognitive Behaviour Therapy

Berni Curwen, Stephen Palmer, Peter Ruddell

SAGE Publications
London • Thousand Oaks • New Delhi

SAGE Publications Ltd
1 Oliver's Yard, 55 City Road
London EC1Y 1SP

SAGE Publications Inc
2455 Teller Road
Thousand Oaks, California 91320

SAGE Publications India Pvt Ltd
B-42 Panchsheel Enclave
PO Box 4109
New Delhi 100 017

British Library Cataloguing in Publication data

A catalogue record for this book is available
from the British Library

ISBN 0 7619 5800 2
ISBN 0 7619 5801 0 (pbk)

Typeset by Mayhew Typesetting, Rhayader, Powys
Printed and bound in Great Britain by Biddles Ltd, King's Lynn, Norfolk

To Julia and Emily (BC and PR)
To Maggie, of course (SP)

Contents

Preface

This book is aimed at practitioners such as counsellors, psychotherapists, and clinical and counselling psychologists who are in
training or are already experienced but wish to learn more about
brief counselling and psychotherapy or wish to continue their professional development. It is hoped this book will be a useful source to
lecturers and trainers of such practitioners, as well as to other helping
professionals such as psychiatrists, mental health nurses, community
mental health nurses, nurse therapists, care managers and others. It
may be of particular help to those working in time-limited settings.

Brief and time-limited therapy is becoming more popular due to the
demands of the marketplace. This has led to an increasing number of
therapists becoming interested in cognitive behaviour therapy and we
hope this book will provide a useful and easily understood
framework. We have found that many therapists and counsellors
who work in time-limited settings and those offering brief therapy
have not received any formal training or read any books devoted to
the subject.

This book will introduce the reader to brief therapy in Chapter 1
and quickly provide a framework for brief cognitive behaviour
therapy. This will be expanded in the whistlestop tour of Chapter 2
where we will first meet Tom, whom we shall follow throughout the
book. We shall also meet other people during the course of the book
who are taken from the authors' clinical practice using dialogue to
illustrate aspects of the framework. Chapter 3 covers the assessment
stage of therapy and gives some guidelines on suitability for brief
cognitive therapy. Although therapy begins in the assessment,
Chapter 4 considers in more detail the beginning stage of therapy by
focusing on the therapist's goals for therapy and the client's difficulties as seen through the cognitive conceptualization. The therapist's
goals and the cognitive conceptualization of the client's difficulties
are continued throughout the process of therapy. Chapter 5 covers
the middle stage of therapy and describes a range of techniques, tools
and interventions used in the practice of brief cognitive behaviour
therapy. Chapter 6 sees the end stage of therapy in which a new
therapist emerges: the client. Chapter 7 includes a number of additional strategies and techniques that can be used within a brief

cognitive behaviour therapy framework. Chapter 8 is devoted to hypnosis as an adjunct to therapy and includes a script which focuses on reframing unhelpful beliefs. Chapter 9 summarizes treatment protocols for the major disorders such as panic and post-traumatic stress disorder (PTSD); also included is suicide.

Terms used

Where pronouns are used, no specific sex is intended: 'he' and 'she' have been used randomly. We have generally used the word 'client' to mean anyone receiving therapy; this is synonymous with 'patient', which may appear in some of the references. We appreciate that some people may object to the use of one or other of these or similar words, preferring other descriptions such as 'user', 'consumer', etc., but we have used client wherever possible for clarity. The term 'therapist' has been used to mean 'psychotherapist', 'counsellor', 'practitioner', etc. We recognize that a debate continues about these titles (see James and Palmer, 1996), but will not develop the arguments further here. We have generally used 'cognitive behaviour therapy' in preference to 'cognitive therapy' or 'cognitive behavioural therapy'. The terms 'cognitive conceptualization', 'case conceptualization' and 'cognitive formulation' have been used interchangeably.

Within the main text, we discuss some aspects of the language we use with clients and emphasize the importance of establishing a (relatively!) common meaning. In the Introduction we note that brief therapy endeavours not to focus on 'deficits', 'weaknesses' and 'pathology'. For these reasons, we have preferred the terms 'helpful' and 'unhelpful' thinking (or beliefs), rather than 'functional' and 'dysfunctional', 'healthy' and 'unhealthy', or 'rational' and 'irrational' thinking (or beliefs). This helps to normalize the client's condition rather than stigmatize their plight. Helpful thinking is therefore seen as what helps a person to achieve their short- and long-term goals and a balance between them. Similarly, we prefer the term 'thinking error', which is part of 'normal' experience (if we accept ourselves as fallible, not perfect, human beings – see Chapter 5), rather than 'cognitive distortion' or 'twisted thinking' (Burns, 1989).

Acknowledgements

We would like to thank Julie Curwen, John Curwen and John Ruddell for supporting Berni and Peter, but especially Julia! We also wish to thank Rosemary Haywood for her help with IT even when inundated with other work. Finally we wish to thank Stephen for giving us the opportunity to co-author this book.

(BC and PR)

1

Introduction

A question commonly asked of people seeking therapy is, 'Why now?' The same question is appropriate to the theme of this book. A question asked by them about therapy is, 'What is it?' This book will tell you what brief cognitive behaviour therapy is. What does 'brief' mean? How long is 'brief'? Does 'brief' apply to the length of the session, the number of sessions, the period of time over which therapy takes place, or to something else? What sort of problems can it be applied to? Are there problems it is not appropriate for?

If unsure what the problem is, would this approach be a good starting point to explore it? Is brief therapy the same as time-limited therapy? Can brief cognitive behaviour therapy stand alone and can it be used in conjunction with other types of therapeutic work?

This chapter will address all of these questions and many others which will emerge as a consequence of doing so. Many of the questions relate to themes which will be more fully considered in the remainder of the book. Clarification of some terms used throughout the rest of the book will be found in the Preface.

Why now?

Several factors have led to a growing demand for brief therapies. Before listing them, it is interesting to note that as long ago as 1946 Alexander and French (1974) directly confronted a number of pivotal analytic dogma current at that time and relating to the length of therapy (Budman and Gurman, 1988: 2):

- that the depth of therapy is necessarily proportionate to the length of treatment and the frequency of interviews;
- that the therapeutic results achieved by a relatively small number of interviews are necessarily superficial and temporary, while therapeutic results achieved by prolonged treatment are necessarily more stable and more profound;
- that the prolongation of an analysis is justified on the grounds that the patient's resistence will eventually be overcome and the desired therapeutic results achieved.

First, and most general, consumerism has reflected that people want their choices met. A growing public awareness of psychotherapy and counselling has begun and continues to develop. In the past, some people have spent years in therapy, often having several sessions each week, and even after several years of such treatment are not well pleased with their progress (see Dinnage, 1988). While some people may require long-term therapy, many want and can benefit from brief therapy. Second (and related to the first point), although in crude terms the amount of psychotherapy being delivered within the NHS has increased, services remain under severe pressure of referrals, with long waiting lists (Parry, 1992). The total amount of time which can be offered by psychotherapists, counsellors, etc. is limited by the system and the effective use of time by these practitioners is obviously important. For example, Newman and Howard (1986: 186) noted that 'the most pervasive myth within the clinical community is that costs are the business of business and not a clinical concern'. Howard et al. (1989) found that 32 per cent of people using psychotherapy services in a long-term setting used 77 per cent of the total sessions available. However, this must be balanced by the recognition that 'psychotherapy researchers legitimately ask different questions to those of service planners and policy makers' (Parry, 1992: 7). Third, purchasers of psychotherapy services seek cost effectiveness or value for money. This applies equally to individuals as to organizational purchasers such as health authorities, the health insurance industry and companies offering employer assisted programmes. Fourth, professionals desiring high service quality and clinical effectiveness look to research and evaluation methods which increasingly point to a treatment of choice for a particular problem range which in many cases is brief (e.g. Milne, 1987; Parry and Watts, 1989; Roth and Fonagy, 1996). Fifth, a number of sources (British Psychological Society, 1990; Grant et al., 1991) suggest that professional interest in the delivery system of psychotherapy services within the NHS serves to protect the interests of particular groups. But research such as the type noted in the fourth point has helped to counter this tendency because when it is undertaken in the clinical setting it combats dogmatic and authoritarian practices (Strupp, 1986).

What is brief therapy?

In this book, brief cognitive behaviour therapy refers to planned brief therapy in which maximum benefits are achieved with the lowest investment of the therapist's time and the lowest cost to the client. Other words used to describe such therapy are, 'short-term', 'time-sensitive', 'time-effective', 'cost-effective', 'abbreviated', 'strategic', 'intermittent', 'episodic', 'limited goal', 'serial' or 'short-term' (see Lazarus and Fay, 1990). 'Time-limited' therapy usually means therapy which has a limited number of sessions and an ending date (Dryden and Feltham, 1992: 3). It may therefore lack the flexibility to enable the evolving cognitive conceptualization of the client's problems (see item 2 of the fundamental characteristics of cognitive behaviour therapy in Chapters 2 and 3) to influence the end point of therapy, in the way that brief therapy does. In practice the distinction between time-limited and brief therapy (as well as other similar terms) is blurred and practitioners may use terms idiosyncratically. However, brief therapy may suggest an initial number of sessions (such as six sessions of 50 minutes) after which progress can be assessed and future sessions planned as required. It is helpful to recognize the distinction between planned brief therapy and brief therapy by default (Budman and Gurman, 1988). Parry (1992: 13) notes that 'most therapy, even as practiced in long-term settings, remains short-term due to attrition (i.e. premature termination of therapy), hence planned short-term therapies may actually result in longer exposure to treatments' (Howard et al., 1986).

Brief therapy as defined at the start of this section implies that time may be used flexibly. Not all sessions have to be of equal length or equally spaced; main sessions may be punctuated by short telephone sessions, for example. Although brief cognitive behaviour therapy may use time flexibly, it always focuses on client goals seen through the framework of the cognitive conceptualization which will be introduced in Chapter 2 and further developed in later chapters. The definition also places no time period on the length of therapy, which may surprise you. However, because people's problems, personalities, life situations, personal styles, problem-solving capacities, intelligence and many other factors vary so much, it is impossible to place a set limit on the length of brief therapy. Budman and Gurman, in their excellent book *Theory and Practice of Brief Therapy* (1988: 5), suggest that 'there is no length in number': the essence of brief therapy is not in numerical time characteristics but in the values, attitudes and aims of the therapist and client'. The general value ideals for any form of brief therapy suggested by these authors are listed below and will be found reflected in the fundamental characteristics of cognitive behaviour therapy outlined in Chapter 2 and in the process of brief cognitive behaviour therapy further detailed in the remainder of the book.

1   Therapy is parsimonious and pragmatic; no attempt is made to remodel the client's basic character; it is assumed that changes in one area of a person's life will spread to other areas.

2   Recognizes a developmental perspective in which significant psychological change is inevitable throughout life (Gilligan, 1982; Neugarten, 1979; Vaillant, 1977). This can be used to therapeutic effect.

3   A person's problems are accepted as such but their individual resources and strengths are acknowledged and utilized in the therapeutic process, rather than focusing on 'deficits', 'weaknesses' and 'pathology'.

4   Many positive changes in the client may occur once therapy has 'finished' and will therefore not be seen by the therapist (see 1 and 7).

5   Effective therapy is not a timeless process; limits will be placed on time.

6   Psychotherapy can be unhelpful if applied unselectively (Frances and Clarkin, 1981: 542).

7   Therapy is a means to an end, not an end in itself: life is more important than therapy!

We have not suggested a set time span for brief therapy and have noted that its essence is in the values, attitudes and aims of the therapist and client. Brief therapists do, in practice, place limits on the overall number of therapy sessions offered and these can vary from one practitioner to another. For example, Malan (1979) has used 30 sessions as a cut-off point, whereas Dryden (1995) has outlined an 11-session protocol; Barkham and Shapiro (1988) and Barkham et al. (1992) developed a three-session format known as the 'two-plus-one' model in which two consecutive weekly sessions are followed three months later by a follow-up session. Talmon (1990) has researched single session therapy (SST). Butcher and Koss (1978) suggest some consensus on 25 sessions for the upper limit of brief therapy.

Some information about the length of therapy may be useful. First, clients on average expect to stay in therapy for between six to ten sessions (Garfield, 1971, 1978). Second, they do stay for an average of six to eight sessions (Garfield, 1978, 1986). Third, it is also in the first six to eight sessions that the major positive impact of psychotherapy occurs (Smith et al., 1980) with continuing but decreasing gains taking place over the next ten sessions, approximately. These results are similar to an earlier meta-analysis by Howard et al. (1986) which indicated that 50 per cent of people improved significantly by the eighth session; 75 per cent by the 26th session; and 83 per cent by the 52nd session. Orlinsky and Howard (1986: 361) note 'a course of diminishing returns with more and more effort required to achieve just noticeable difference in patient improvement'. The brief cognitive behaviour therapist, consistent with item one in the above list, does not seek a complete character change in the client, but sufficient improvement for better engagement with life in which further gains may ensue (see items 4 and 7). Teasdale et al. (1984) and Scott (1992) found that the cognitive model is quickly assimilated by some clients who found even very short interventions helpful.

Who will benefit?

Chapter 3 of this book – assessment – considers some of the types of problems and some of the characteristics of the people experiencing these problems which will help you to decide whether or not to offer brief cognitive behaviour therapy to a particular person seeking it, or seeking therapy in general. We also note in Chapter 3 some of the problem areas in which research has been conducted and for which cognitive behaviour therapy has been shown to be effective. Nevertheless, we believe that the cognitive model outlined in Chapter 2 is a sufficiently general model of psychological functioning to enable it to be applied to most psychological problem areas, albeit with some adaptation. As will be noted in the text, cognitive behaviour therapy imports techniques and tools into therapy, provided these are consistent with the overall model.

In considering who will benefit from brief cognitive behaviour therapy, an important question for the therapist to ask herself is: 'Might this person gain substantially from this form of therapy or would another therapy, of similar or longer duration, or work with another therapist be more suitable?' Lazarus (1989) suggests that a person's suitability for certain orientations of therapy or therapeutic modalities indicated to be of most use to them is best assessed from the start. Brewin and Bradley (1989) argue that clients may have a better outcome in their preferred therapeutic orientation and that some outcome research is flawed by failing to take this into account. Wanigarante and Barker (1995) found in a study of therapeutic styles conducted in a day hospital setting that 'overall, the cognitive-behavioural style was the most preferred' when compared to psychodynamic, humanistic, external and naive styles.

In Chapter 2 and elsewhere, we emphasize the importance of the therapeutic relationship. Parloff et al. (1978) provide some evidence to suggest that therapist–client compatibility on a variety of personality characteristics is an important component of the quality of this relationship. A dilemma facing you will be that the characteristics given in the assessment chapter indicating suitability for short-term cognitive behaviour therapy may be similar to the factors indicating suitability for long-term therapy (e.g. see Levin, 1962; Zetzel, 1968). Although we outline a number of factors indicating suitability for short-term cognitive behaviour therapy, the science is still young and pragmatism is necessary. Some therapists advocate allocating one to three therapy sessions (or pretherapy trial) to ascertain a client's suitability (Budman, 1981; Budman and Clifford, 1979; Budman et al., 1981; Sachs, 1983). Feltham (1997: 54), drawing on the work of Garfield (1995) and Cummings and Sayama (1995), suggests that 'the best we can aim for is practitioners who are honest, conscientious, flexible and experienced enough to offer each client suitably individualised counselling'.

We posed the question above: 'Might this person gain substantially from this form of therapy or would another therapy, of similar or longer duration, or work with another therapist be more suitable?' In attempting to answer this question, two further questions arise. Can brief cognitive behaviour therapy stand alone and can it be used in conjunction with other types of therapeutic work? For a number of people and their problems, brief cognitive behaviour therapy will be all that is necessary to bring about sufficient change and it is assumed this will continue beyond therapy; both between sessions and after therapy has 'ended' (see item one above). Brief cognitive behaviour therapy is pragmatic and may be used in conjunction with other treatments: abbreviated therapy for depression (Scott et al., 1994) and partial hospitalization (Block and Lefkovitz, 1991) are examples of practice in which brief cognitive behaviour therapy has been used alongside drug therapy. The Pennsylvania Center for Cognitive Therapy suggests that a client may sometimes benefit by combining individual therapy with couple therapy, group therapy and self-help groups (see Ruddell and Curwen, 1997).

When does it end?

Brief cognitive behaviour therapy does not seek to remodel the client's basic character (see item one above) and recognizes a developmental process (see item 2 above). Some therapists believe that a primary care model is appropriate to psychotherapy and counselling, where the client is seen for a number of intermittent courses of therapy over their lifetime using different techniques and interventions (Budman and Gurman, 1988; Cummings, 1990; Cummings and Sayama, 1995). Such brief intermittent psychotherapy throughout the life cycle, also referred to as episodic or serial short-term therapy, recognizes that psychotherapy need not attempt to restructure the personality and often fails to prevent further psychological problems in life which may arise from the developmental process or distressing life situations. We consider this model to be compatible with brief cognitive behaviour therapy, while recognizing that it could be unhelpful if provided unselectively (see item 6 above).

Keeping it brief!

The Preface has outlined the shape of this book. Two points may help you to practise brief therapy:

1 Familiarize yourself with the fundamental characteristics of cognitive behaviour therapy (Chapter 2).
2 Use the cognitive conceptualization (see Chapter 3) to keep focused throughout therapy.

2

The Cognitive-Behavioural Framework

A whistlestop tour

This chapter will briefly outline the basic principles and practices of cognitive behaviour therapy. A central principle of cognitive behaviour therapy is that thoughts, emotions, behaviours and physiology are part of a unified system. A change to any one part will be accompanied by changes to the other parts. For example, if a person's television exploded as she watched it, she may experience immediate physiological changes (a surge of adrenalin); a rapid shift of behaviour (from calmly watching the screen to rushing for a fire blanket or to telephone for help); a feeling of anxiety and thoughts or cognitions such as '!*!*!*: the house is burning – I'm going to die'. Cognitive behaviour therapy recognizes the unified nature of this process. The scenario presented here does not represent a psychological problem, but where psychological problems exist, change is sought through focus on unhelpful thoughts. It is important to stress that components such as emotions and behaviours are not ignored or considered unimportant and we will demonstrate in later chapters how these are given full consideration in a process which brings about therapeutic change.

In reading about the exploding television, you may have thought that you would not have experienced a rush of adrenalin or felt or acted in the same way. Cognitive behaviour therapy accounts for this by suggesting that each person brings to a situation a different range of feelings, physiological responses and behaviours and that thoughts guide these. Feelings and responses are not caused intrinsically by the situation itself, but largely by the way in which each of us views it. This was realized at least as long ago as the first century AD when the stoic philosopher Epictetus noted that people 'are disturbed not by things but by the views which they take of them'. In the present century a number of professionals have taken a similar view: Arnold (1960); Beck (1964); Ellis (1962); Kelly (1955); Lazarus (1966).

Beck developed cognitive therapy and his work initially centred on depression (1963). The central themes of cognitive behaviour therapy are:

- that thoughts can lead to emotions and behaviour;
- that emotional disorders arise from negatively biased thinking (which leads to unhelpful emotions and behaviour);
- that emotional disorders can be helped by changing such thinking (which is assumed to be learned).

Two components of thinking are focused upon in cognitive behaviour therapy: automatic thoughts and underlying beliefs.

Automatic thoughts
Automatic thoughts was a term given by Beck to the thoughts and images which occur involuntarily in a person's stream of consciousness (Beck and Greenberg, 1974). Similar terms are 'internalized statements', 'self-statements' or 'things you tell yourself' (Ellis, 1962), 'self-talk' (Maultsby, 1968).

Underlying beliefs
These are the beliefs and assumptions which generate the thoughts and images forming the content of automatic thoughts. The relationship between automatic thoughts and underlying beliefs can be better understood by briefly considering the idea of schemas. Schemas are abstract mental plans that serve as guides to action, as structures for remembering and interpreting information and as organized frameworks for solving problems. Each of us adopts a vast range of schemas which allow us to make sense of the world and to place any new information or experiences into context (for example, see Rumelhart, 1981; Rumelhart and Ortony, 1977; Rosen, 1988). They are like vast filing systems which each of us uses to order the world and which begin to be formed from early childhood. Once formed, they guide information processing and behaviour (Bartlett, 1932) and shape how a person thinks, feels and behaves concerning self, others and the world. Importantly, they are hierarchical. For example, matter can be perceived as animate or inanimate; animals as vertebrates or invertebrates and so on (see Figure 2.1).

Similarly, in the case of the exploding television, a person who holds an underlying belief (i.e. a belief further up the hierarchy) such as 'fire always causes death' is likely to feel panic stricken and beset with automatic thoughts such as 'I am going to die', accompanied by negative images such as a charred body engulfed by fire. The person who holds the belief that 'fire is dangerous if not controlled' may feel sufficient concern to act appropriately and may experience automatic thoughts such as 'cut the electrics – get help now', accompanied by helpful and constructive coping imagery. A person who holds a belief at the top of the hierarchy, such as 'life is dangerous', will be

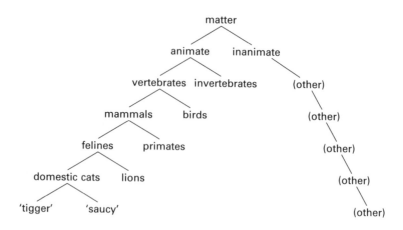

Figure 2.1   *Schema representation*

predisposed to anxiety in a wide range of situations. A belief such as this, at the top of an hierarchy and affecting a large portion of a person's life is known as a core belief. We follow Beck's view that the schema is the cognitive structure (or 'filing system') within the mind, whereas the core belief is the specific content (Beck, 1964); but a number of practitioners use the two terms interchangeable (Padesky, 1994). Core beliefs operate at a rudimentary level and are global, rigid and overgeneralized.

Intermediate beliefs
Between core beliefs and automatic thoughts lie a number of intermediate beliefs (Figure 2.2). Intermediate beliefs are composed of attitudes, rules and assumptions:

- *Attitude*: it is dreadful to be in danger.
- *Rule* (expectation): I must always be safe and act with caution.
- *Assumption*: if I always act with caution life will be less dangerous.

We have briefly outlined the cognitive structures that hold the key to psychological difficulties which individuals experience. How does a cognitive behaviour therapist help a client to overcome these difficulties through brief therapy? Obviously, basic counselling skills are a prerequisite and are identified by Truax and Carkhuff (1967) as follows:

1   Be accurately empathic.
2   Be 'with' the client.

Core beliefs	Intermediate beliefs	Automatic thoughts
Global	Attitudes	Stream of thought
Rigid	Rules/expectations	Images
Overgeneralized	Assumptions	Words/phrases

Figure 2.2 *Schemas*

3   Be understanding, or grasp the client's meaning.
4   Communicate empathic understanding.
5   Communicate unconditional positive regard.

While these are basic counselling skills, there are a number of characteristics fundamental to cognitive behaviour therapy which enable the therapist to help the client by explaining, exploring and building upon the principle of thoughts leading to feelings and behaviours and some bodily reactions, as described above. Some therapists find it useful to symbolize this principle as ABC (Ellis, 1962, 1977), where A means Activating event, B means Belief and C means Consequence:

- A   *Activating event*: television exploding.
- B   *Belief*: I'm in grave danger.
- C   *Consequence*: anxiety.

The A (activating event) may be an actual event such as the exploding television, an experience or even a thought, daydream, image or emotion about which a person might have thoughts or beliefs. The B (belief) may be a core belief, an underlying assumption, an intermediate belief or an automatic thought. 'Many times, maladaptive ideation occurs in a pictorial form instead of, or in addition to, the verbal form' (Beck, 1970). The C (consequence) may be anything the thought or belief (B) leads to, such as an emotion (fear), a behaviour (running away) or a physiological response (palpitations).

Cognitive behaviour therapy progressively encourages the client to recognize and accept their emotions, to detect first their automatic thoughts and then the related underlying beliefs (both intermediate and core). Only if the connection between thoughts (beliefs) and emotions (consequences) is recognized can further progress be made through cognitive behaviour therapy. Once this process is started the client is encouraged to look for evidence in support of unreasonable and unhelpful beliefs. The inability to find such evidence poses a challenge to such unhelpful beliefs, which are in turn transformed into more adaptive, helpful beliefs. These new and more realistic beliefs no longer support the distressing emotions and behaviours. To aid this process, an *automatic thought form* is commonly used (see item 7, p. 21, and Figure 2.7, p. 27). Beliefs and emotions are rated to aid belief change and evaluation over time (see scaling beliefs, p. 80).

Thinking errors

Thinking errors are also known as cognitive distortions or twisted thinking (Burns, 1980, 1989). Identifying automatic thoughts and recognizing the thinking errors contained within them plays a major role within cognitive behaviour therapy. Individual clients tend to make consistent errors in their thinking. The therapist helps the client to identify these errors or cognitive distortions. Clients are introduced to the notion that when people feel emotionally distressed they often have accompanying thoughts which seem believable at the time but which on closer scrutiny are not always consistent with objective reality and are unhelpful to the client. Most of the negative thoughts which disturb a client are distorted and unrealistic. A client will be taught how to identify the thinking errors which lead to negative moods. It is important to convey to the client that they are not alone in having these distortions. They are common to human-kind but proliferate with emotional distress. We identify the most common thinking errors in Figure 2.3.

1   All or nothing thinking (also known as dichotomous thinking)
This is where a client evaluates herself, other people, situations and the world in extreme categories. This type of thinking tends to be absolutist and does not allow for shades of grey. An example is the young mother who views herself as all bad because she becomes frustrated with her young child and views other mothers as always being patient with their children. So she sees other mothers as all good and herself as all bad, which is unrealistic.

2   Personalization and blame
Personalization is a thinking error in which a person totally blames herself for all that goes wrong and relates this to some deficiency or inadequacy in herself. She holds herself personally responsible for an event which is not entirely under her control. An example is the young trainee who believes her trainer is brusque with her because she made a mistake. She overlooks the part others may play and confuses the possibility that she may have contributed to what happened but

```
1   All or nothing thinking
2   Personalization and blame
3   Catastrophizing
4   Emotional reasoning
5   Should or must statements
6   Mental filter (selective abstraction)
7   Disqualifying or discounting the positive
8   Overgeneralization
9   Magnification and minimization
10  Labelling
11  Jumping to conclusions (arbitrary inference)
    •  Mind reading
    •  Fortune telling
```

Figure 2.3   *Thinking errors*

was not totally responsible. The opposite is to blame others. She blames others for her problems or circumstances and does not believe she has contributed to the problem. An example is the woman who totally blames her husband for the break-up of their marriage.

3   Catastrophizing (fortune telling)
This is where the person predicts the future negatively and believes things will turn out badly. This thinking error is common with anxiety problems (Ellis, 1962) where clients tend to dwell on the worst possible outcome of any situation. An example is the successful manager about to make a presentation for the company. He becomes preoccupied with thoughts that he will make a mess of his presentation, let down his company, lose his job and become destitute.

4   Emotional reasoning
This is where a person draws conclusions about an event based entirely upon their feelings and ignoring any evidence to the contrary. For example, the young man who has been waiting thirty minutes for his new partner to arrive feels sad and rejected. He says to himself 'I've been ditched' and fails to consider that his partner may have been delayed at work, missed the bus, got a flat tyre, etc.

5   Should or must statements
This is where the person has a fixed idea of how she, others or the world 'should' or 'must' be. Preferences or expectations are elevated to rigid demands. When these demands are not met the person feels emotionally distressed and overestimates how bad it is that her expectations have not been met. For example, the gymnast

performing a difficult manoeuvre on the parallel bars said to herself, 'I really shouldn't have made so many mistakes.' This led to her feeling so angry and frustrated with herself that she did not practise for many days.

6 Mental filter (selective abstraction)

The person pays particular attention to one negative detail and dwells on it endlessly, regardless of any other positive aspects. She does not view the picture as a whole and concentrates on the one negative aspect. For example, a young woman receives many positive comments about her new hairstyle from friends, but one friend said she did not like that particular style. She had this comment on her mind for days and wore a hat.

7 Disqualifying or discounting the positive

This is where the client ignores the positive of any situation and tells himself that these positive experiences do not count. For example, a man produces excellent meals on most occasions, but does not give himself any praise. He produced a nourishing but unappetising meal on one occasion and thought of himself as being an awful and unimaginative cook.

8 Overgeneralization

The person thinks that because an unpleasant experience happened to him once, it will always happen. This is where he makes sweeping generalized conclusions on the basis of one situation. The man who attended a job interview but did not get the position believed he would be rejected for every job.

9 Magnification and minimization

The person who makes this thinking error when evaluating herself, other people or situations will tend to exaggerate or magnify the negative components and minimize or play down the positive. When being appraised at work she overestimates the importance of some areas where change is needed and pays little attention to a considerable range of positive aspects highlighted by the appraisal. She concludes that this shows how inadequate she is.

10 Labelling

This is where the person views herself or others in all or nothing terms but goes beyond this by applying a label which is usually derogatory. For example, the mother we referred to in item 1 might label herself 'a heartless bitch'. When this thinking error is applied to others a client dislikes or disagrees with, he may say to himself, 'He's an arse.' The client will see the person as globally bad and may then feel angry and hostile. The client who makes an error at work may label herself as 'totally stupid'.

11   Jumping to conclusions (arbitrary inference)

A person whose thinking is distorted in this way infers that a particular outcome will be negative, without having any evidence, or even if the evidence points to a positive outcome. There are two main types of this thinking error:

1   **Mind reading**
    The client thinks she knows what others are thinking and does not consider other more plausible or likely possibilities. An example would be the client with social anxiety who thinks her work colleagues see her as inadequate in a wide range of situations.
2   **Fortune telling**
    A person predicts that events in the future will turn out badly. For example, a person attending for a routine chest X-ray assumes he has cancer (see catastrophizing, where fortune telling is greatly exaggerated).

Clusters of thinking errors

It is important to note that a particular automatic thought, belief, or inference may contain not one, but several of these thinking errors and we will exemplify this later. In introducing these thinking errors, we noted that an individual may tend to make consistent errors in their thinking. For example, a particular person may frequently use a cluster such as jumping to conclusions, 'should' statements, emotional reasoning and magnification/minimization. Similarly, emotional problems such as anxiety, depression or guilt each tend to have a prominent cluster of cognitive distortions or thinking errors surrounding them. Figure 2.4 gives the clusters of thinking errors common to particular emotional problems. This can be used as an aid to help the therapist to identify the most significant thinking errors for a particular problem. However, it is important to note that the clusters which a particular individual brings to a specific emotional problem will frequently have an idiosyncratic element.

Fundamental characteristics of cognitive behaviour therapy

So far in this chapter, we have outlined the mechanisms by which a person experiences emotional difficulties or distress. In the next section we will guide you through the fundamental characteristics of

	Anxiety panic, nervousness	Depression	Anger	Guilt	Hurt	Morbid jealousy	Shame/ embarrassment
All or nothing thinking	✓	✓	✓		✓		✓
Personalization/blame		✓	✓	✓			✓
Catastrophizing	✓	✓				✓	✓
Emotional reasoning	✓	✓	✓	✓	✓	✓	
'Should' or 'must' statements	✓	✓		✓	✓	✓	
Mental filter		✓				✓	✓
Discounting the positive	✓	✓					
Overgeneralization	✓	✓	✓				
Magnification/minimization	✓	✓	✓	✓	✓		
Labelling			✓				✓
Jumping to conclusions							
(a) Mind reading	✓	✓	✓		✓	✓	✓
(b) Fortune telling	✓	✓					✓

Figure 2.4   *Thinking errors for common problems*

1	Therapeutic style
2	Formulation of problem
3	Collaborative relationship
4	Structure to sessions and to therapy
5	Goal-directed therapy
6	Examines and questions unhelpful thinking
7	Uses range of aids and techniques
8	Teaches client to become own therapist
9	Homework setting
10	Time limited
11	Audio-recording sessions

Figure 2.5   *Fundamental characteristics of cognitive behaviour therapy*

cognitive behaviour therapy by which this model is applied to the client's problems. Figure 2.5 is a list of the fundamental characteristics of cognitive behaviour therapy.

1   Therapeutic style
We start with therapeutic style because this is often quite different in cognitive behaviour therapy to some other forms of counselling. In cognitive behaviour therapy, it is assumed that the therapist brings to the therapeutic encounter a range of skills and knowledge. From this it follows that the therapist, particularly in the early stages of therapy, directs the course of therapy. The therapist's style is therefore active and directive. The therapist is sensitive to balance this with communicating empathic understanding and being 'with' the client, together with grasping the client's meaning (see items 2, 3, 4, pp. 12–13). Part of this style is about the ability to elicit information appropriate to the client's problems that will include the client's cognitions.

2   Formulation of problem
The therapist gathers a wide range of information about the client and her problems. This is based not only on verbal information from the client but from the therapist's own observations. A full assessment is carried out early on in therapy (discussed more fully in a later chapter) and a *cognitive formulation* or *conceptualization* of the client's problems is made. This is constantly revised in the light of new information. In particular, the therapist identifies current thinking associated with and maintaining problematic behaviours and emotions, *precipitating factors* connected to the current problem and reinforcing unhelpful beliefs, and the client's unhelpful interpretation

of major developmental events. The cognitive conceptualization is more fully discussed in Chapter 3.

3 Collaborative relationship

The therapist is open about his formulation and usually shares it with the client at some point for discussion together and for further development. Unlike some forms of therapy, cognitive behaviour therapy is transparent and does not present therapy as magical, but is psychoeducational and informs the client (in easily understood language) about the process of therapy. To this end reading material (i.e. bibliotherapy) is often used (Lazarus, 1971; Macaskill and Macaskill, 1991). The therapist socializes the client into such aspects as recognizing automatic thoughts and other unhelpful beliefs, and recommending certain courses of action such as homework, but encourages the client to participate fully and to take over responsibility for many aspects of therapy from an early stage.

The openness of therapy is further aided by client and therapist setting an agenda together for each session, as well as giving and receiving feedback. Through such collaboration and by using other therapeutic skills not specific to cognitive behaviour therapy (outlined above), the therapist quickly establishes a therapeutic relationship with the client. With some clients who have deep and far-reaching psychological problems (as may be the case when working with people with personality disorders) it may be necessary to take more time and care in ensuring this is firmly established before entering too far into therapy, as outlined elsewhere in this chapter. Where this is so, brief therapy may not be appropriate unless a discrete and limited problem area is being worked with (see Beck et al., 1990a).

4 Structure to sessions and to therapy

As discussed in the last section, sessions are structured by an agenda, the contents of which is collaboratively agreed upon by therapist and client. The agenda has a common format applied across all sessions except the first. Although it need not be slavishly adhered to, the novice therapist is best advised to follow it during their course of training. The use of the agenda has several benefits which become more pronounced in brief therapy. It allows the client and therapist to use their limited time most efficiently. It helps to ensure that important material which client or therapist wish to bring to the session is not left to the end or entirely forgotten. It also aids collaboration by encouraging a problem-solving and business-like attitude (rather than encouraging a 'patient' or 'sick' role). The agenda also provides a convenient framework for monitoring progress throughout therapy.

It gives a structure to help the client to understand the central themes of cognitive behaviour therapy and to apply this structure to herself once therapy is terminated. The structure of a typical session is as follows:

1   Check client's mood.
2   Brief review of week.
3   Set agenda for current session.
4   Feedback, and link to, previous session.
5   Review homework.
6   Discuss agenda items.
7   Set homework.
8   Seek feedback at end of session.

The structure of therapy has a number of elements which are concerned with effectiveness and efficiency. These elements of cognitive behaviour therapy are relatively constant over its course, but some aspects change as therapy progresses. Cognitive behaviour therapy recognizes that different stages are involved and optimizes this development by incorporating relevant tasks and responsibilities (for client and therapist) at the pertinent stage. For example, identifying automatic thoughts will be central to the start of therapy while modifying core beliefs will usually not be attempted until later in the process. The structuring of therapy in this way allows for the termination of therapy, relapse prevention and booster sessions to be planned in advance and obstacles to be confronted and overcome. The structure of therapy will also be determined by the particular problem with which the client presents. For example, if a client is diagnosed in accordance with the fourth edition of the *Diagnostic and Statistical Manual of Mental Disorders* (DSM-IV) of the American Psychiatric Association (1994) as having bulimia nervosa, the three-phase structure of therapy suggested by Fairburn and Cooper (1989) may be followed.

5   Goal-directed therapy
We have already described the way in which the therapist and client collaboratively work together. When the client brings material to the session, the therapist encourages her to put this into behavioural terms. For example, if the client says that she feels depressed, the therapist will check out with her how this depression manifests itself in her. If she says, among other aspects, that she now seldom socializes, that she no longer keeps a healthy diet or that she has abandoned activities that she previously found enjoyable, the re-establishment of these tasks may become specific goals for therapy. Similarly, anyone who seeks therapy seeks change in some way: the therapist will work

collaboratively with the client to decide on the changes which are germane to therapy. Goals will be decided upon collaboratively, together with the tasks necessary to bring about such goals. There may be occasions when the client initially wants to achieve a goal which is counterproductive to her progress; for example, where she seeks goals consistent with the unrealistic belief that she must be perfect in every way. In such cases, the therapist will discuss this frankly with her. It is only through appropriate goal setting that brief therapy is possible. Realistically, brief cognitive behaviour therapy is 'limited goal therapy' (see Lazarus and Fay, 1990) and if a client has many therapeutic goals then he or she may be unsuited to a brief intervention.

6   *Examines and questions unhelpful thinking*

The cornerstone of cognitive behaviour therapy is that thoughts guide behaviour, emotions and (in some cases) physiological responses. A person will need to alter their thinking if they are to overcome various psychological problems. Depending on the nature of the problem, this may entail working on automatic thoughts, intermediate thoughts or core beliefs. Unlike some forms of cognitive therapy such as rational emotive behaviour therapy – REBT (Ellis, 1994), cognitive behaviour therapy does not confront unhelpful thinking head on, but uses a process of socratic questioning whereby the client is encouraged to look at the evidence for holding his unhelpful (unrealistic or negative) beliefs (Beck et al., 1979: 66–71). It is important to check out the meaning of a client's beliefs before attempting to work on them. This becomes particularly important when working across cultures (Ruddell, 1997: 22–4). Another major difference between rational emotive behaviour therapy and cognitive behaviour therapy is that the latter works mainly at an inferential level during the beginning stage of therapy while REBT works mostly at an evaluative level. For example, consider the person mentioned when we viewed catastrophizing (p. 13). The successful manager drew the inference that he would 'make a mess' of his presentation. The cognitive behaviour therapist may invite him to look at the evidence for this inference; if the evidence was lacking, this would remove the foundations on which his other beliefs (about letting his company down, losing his job and becoming destitute) are founded. However, the rational emotive behaviour therapist would prefer to focus on the evaluations which may ensue from such an inference such as 'I must not make a mess of the presentation, and if I did, I couldn't stand it.'

A list of questions about thoughts and beliefs from which the therapist may draw has been developed by Palmer and Dryden (1995) and Palmer and Strickland (1996). They are reproduced in

- Is it logical?
- Would a scientist agree with your logic?
- Where is the evidence for your belief?
- Where is the belief written (apart from inside your own head!)?
- Is your belief realistic?
- Would your friends and colleagues agree with your idea?
- Does everybody share your attitude? If not, why not?
- Are you expecting yourself or others to be perfect as opposed to fallible human beings?
- What makes the situation so terrible, awful or horrible?
- Are you making a mountain out of a molehill?
- Will it seem this bad in one, three, six or twelve months' time?
- Will it be important in two years' time?
- Are you exaggerating the importance of this problem?
- Are you fortune telling with little evidence that the worst case scenario will actually happen?
- If you 'can't stand it' or 'can't bear it' what will really happen?
- If you 'can't stand it' will you really fall apart?
- Are you concentrating on your own (or others') weaknesses and neglecting strengths?
- Are you agonizing about how you think things should be instead of dealing with them as they are?
- Where is this thought or attitude getting you?
- Is your belief helping you to attain your goals?
- Is your belief goal focused and problem solving?
- If a friend made a similar mistake, would you be so critical?
- Are you thinking in all-or-nothing terms: is there any middle ground?
- Are you *labelling* yourself, somebody or something else? Is this logical and a fair thing to do?
- Just because a problem has occurred does it mean that you/they/it are 'stupid', 'a failure', 'useless' or 'hopeless'?
- Are you placing rules on yourself or others (e.g. shoulds or musts, etc.)? If so, are they proving helpful and constructive?
- Are you taking things too personally?
- Are you blaming others unfairly just to make yourself (temporarily) feel better?

Figure 2.6   *Questions to help examine unhelpful thinking*

Figure 2.6 and are best used in the context of the process of cognitive behaviour therapy outlined throughout this book. They are shown as Appendix 1 in an altered form as a list of questions which the client may ask herself as a *self-help aid.*

7   *Uses range of aids and techniques*
We have already noted that a central task of the cognitive behaviour therapist is to arrive at a cognitive conceptualization of the client's

problems. The conceptualization, which may be developed over time, guides the course of therapy. This leaves the therapist reasonably free to import a range of techniques and aids to help bring about a change in the client's unhelpful thinking, which will in turn lead to the client overcoming his emotional and behavioural problems. However, any such techniques and aids are firmly embedded within the framework and principles of cognitive behaviour therapy rather than being 'add ons'. An example of a technique is the use of behavioural experiments with panic disordered clients, such as voluntary hyperventilation (Clark, 1986). Aids include a wide range of instruments – questionnaires – (see Ruddell, 1997) to measure aspects of a client's problem, such as Rapid Assessment Instruments (RAIs; see Corcoran and Fischer, 1987). Probably the most commonly used aid in cognitive behaviour therapy is the Beck Depression Inventory (BDI; Beck et al., 1961; Beck and Steer, 1987). Another aid is the *automatic thought form*, of which there are many variations. Our own form (completed) is shown in Figure 2.7 (p. 27) and discussed previously (p. 12). A blank version is shown as Appendix 2.

8   *Teach client to become own therapist*
One of the main reasons cognitive behaviour therapy is open, structured, collaborative, relatively brief, goal directed and uses homework is to hand over the process of bringing about change to the client before therapy is terminated. The scope and fluency of the skills the client learns will depend in part on the nature and severity of the client's problem, which in turn will influence the length of therapy. A crucial factor in the client becoming his own therapist is his active participation in the process of therapy within formal sessions as well as in assignments outside them.

9   *Homework setting*
The average length of a therapeutic session is about one hour. If a client only focuses on his problems during the session, this means that within a week 167 hours will not be put to good therapeutic use. In turn, this leads to a lack of continuity in working with a particular problem because the therapeutic process of recording, monitoring and assessing thoughts will not be easily carried into daily living. A useful analogy here is that of maintaining physical health: people do not usually object to cleaning their teeth, bathing, washing their hair regularly and so on – in just the same way it is important to allot time to maintaining our mental health. A problem sometimes encountered with the setting of 'homework' is the word itself. Some people connect it with schoolwork which in turn may have negative

associations. It is important to check this out with a client and if this is the only obstacle, to use a term – preferably chosen by him – which does not have such negative connotations. 'Assignment' is a commonly used alternative. In passing, such thoughts can be used as therapeutic material. A further reason for clients to continue their work outside sessions is that it is sometimes not until they are in the midst of a particular situation, or type of situation, that they are able to capture their most salient automatic thoughts – sometimes known as 'hot cognitions'. Another important reason for homework is that it more ably equips the client with the means to continue therapy alone once the sessions come to an end, since he will already have developed a degree of proficiency from carrying out homework assignments. Assignments vary enormously, depending on the client, the problem and the stage of therapy. A common assignment is to complete an automatic thought form.

10   Time limited

Time constraints have been more fully discussed in Chapter 1 in relation to brief cognitive behaviour therapy. We wish only to add here that cognitive behaviour therapy is limited in time, compared to many other approaches, due to its directive, collaborative, goal-directed and structured approach.

11   Audio recording sessions

The practice of audio recording sessions is not central to cognitive behaviour therapy but it is often carried out and can be useful for the following reasons. First, it can be helpful for supervision and may provide the supervisor with different and more detailed primary information about the session than the secondary description given by the (trainee) therapist possibly after some time has elapsed. As with other aspects of cognitive behaviour therapy, audio taping is carried out with the collaboration of the client, alongside a discussion of the reasons for use of the tape. Second, the client may benefit from recording the session himself as it enables him to revisit aspects of the session at home. This reinforces the practice of working therapeutically both inside and outside the session (see *homework setting*, p. 22), contributes to the *openness* of therapy (see *collaborative relationship*, p. 18) and helps enable clients to develop therapeutic skills which they can apply to their own problems (see *teach client to become own therapist*, p. 22).

The following extract is taken from a typical session. The dialogue will be interrupted with a commentary indicating the points at which the factors above, the *fundamental characteristics of cognitive behaviour therapy*, are demonstrated. The therapist and client have already greeted each other and both have set their audiotapes in motion for the session.

> *Therapist:* How have you been feeling this week, Tom?
> *Client:* It's not been so bad the last couple of days, but at the weekend, I went right down again – back to square one.
> *Therapist:* So it seems like your mood has been quite up and down . . .
> *Client:* Hmm.
> *Therapist:* Can we put that on the agenda to look at in more detail?
> *Client:* Yeah.

Even from this brief extract, taken from the start of a session, some of the characteristics of cognitive behaviour therapy are in evidence. The therapist commences by checking the client's mood and will shortly move on briefly to review the client's week. These are the first components in the structure of a typical session as discussed in the fourth fundamental characteristic, *structure to sessions and to therapy* (p. 18). It is also apparent that the therapist is interacting with the client and demonstrates the directive quality of his therapeutic style by focusing on agenda setting (see *1 Therapeutic style*, p. 17). However, the therapist tempers this directive aspect by eliciting feedback from the client which helps in establishing a *collaborative relationship* (p. 18).

> *Therapist:* Could I see your depression inventory? [*Client hands therapist a Beck Depression Inventory (BDI) completed prior to the session.*]
> *Therapist:* Thanks . . . Is there anything else that happened during the week that you would like to talk about today?
> *Client:* The weekend was awful. Kas started on at me and things went from bad to worse . . .
> *Therapist:* Okay. We've put what happened at the weekend on the agenda. Before we set the rest of the agenda, I'd briefly like to ask you about last week's session – what stands out in your mind about it?
> *Client:* Well, it was a relief to find out that I can do something about my problems after all this time and that they're all connected. In a way, that made it seem more manageable. Also, the forms you gave me helped me to see that the way I think about things can make my problems worse, so if I start to think about things in a different way I could start to feel better. It was helpful to have this jotted in my notebook as a reminder.

The therapist regularly monitors the client's mood throughout the course of therapy as well as within individual sessions. As noted under *7 Uses range of aids and techniques* (p. 21), the therapist commonly uses the Beck Depression Inventory (BDI) to monitor the client's mood. Many therapists arrange for the client to complete appropriate inventories in the waiting area immediately prior to commencing a session, as the therapist in the extract above demonstrates. The client also alludes to two aids: a therapy notebook and an automatic thought form (see Figure 2.7). In brief cognitive behaviour therapy, clients are encouraged to keep a therapy notebook in which salient details of the session are noted and points outside the session which the client believes are important. An important aspect of the therapy notebook is to link the sessions together and to link therapy with other parts of the client's life. The automatic thought form was used by Tom as part of an assignment following the last session (see *9 Homework setting*, p. 22). Although the client in this extract says that the forms helped him to link his thoughts and feelings together, this was a theme already discussed in some detail when the client's problems were initially formulated (see *2 Formulation of problem*, p. 17) and initial goals for therapy set (see *5 Goal-directed therapy*, p. 19). The client's 'insight' of linking thoughts and feelings as a result of working with automatic thought forms outside the session is one of the benefits of the psychoeducational approach adopted by cognitive behaviour therapy. This is also an early stage in the development of the client learning to work independently of the therapist (see *8 Teach client to become own therapist*, p. 22). The extract also sees the therapist following a typical session structure by moving on to set an agenda (see *4 Structure to sessions and to therapy*, p. 18).

Therapist: I'm glad you've been so quick to make the link between thoughts and feelings. That's a really important part of this work . . . Did you find anything in the last session that troubled you?

Client: No, not once I got here!

Therapist: [*laughs*] Is there anything else that happened during the week that you would like to include on today's agenda?

Client: No, I don't think so.

Therapist: Right. And is there anything else you would like to put on today's agenda?

Client: No . . . Only what we said I'd try out during the week. I didn't manage to do it all.

Therapist: Okay, shall we put last week's homework on the agenda too, and spend some time looking at the difficulties you had in completing it?

Client: Yeah, okay.

Therapist: You might remember me saying that we will usually look at the work you've done outside of the sessions, with me during the session?

Client: That's right.

Therapist: That's most of our agenda set for today. Do you recall what else we usually have on the agenda too?

Client: I suppose we need some time to look at things I can do . . . like the forms I did last week . . .

Therapist: Your assignment?

Client: Yeah, that's it.

Therapist: Okay, and we can allocate some time to set the coming week's assignments and can finish by looking at your thoughts and feelings about this session. Can we move straight on to look at your assignments? You said that you hadn't been able to complete it all.

Client: That's right. I did three of the sheets before the weekend, but after our big row I felt really down and didn't feel up to doing any more.

Therapist: You said earlier that the forms you took away with you were helpful in letting you make a link between the feelings you had and the thoughts that triggered them and I'd like to carry that forward to how your thoughts and feelings about your row with Kas led to you being unable to carry on with the work you had started and had found helpful up to that point . . . Do you want to look at the work you have done first, or would you prefer to focus on the difficulties you had that prevented you from doing the rest?

Client: Well, after we had the row, it was like all the stuff I'd done up to that point got wiped out . . . and it made the work with the forms seem meaningless. So I guess I'd like to look at that part first.

Therapist: Okay. You said the work you had done up to that point had got 'wiped out' and you also said earlier that you had completed three of the *automatic thought forms*. Can I check this out with you? Would you think of a time shortly before you had the row with Kas . . . Can you let me know whether or not the work with the forms was useful up to that point?

Client: Yeah, as I said earlier, I did find it helpful linking the thoughts and feelings and was feeling quite optimistic but when we had the row it just counted for nothing.

Therapist: When you were using the forms, part of your assignment was to identify disturbing feelings and link these with particular thoughts. Do you recall if the form asked you to identify anything else?

Client: [*looking at homework*] What, the alternative thoughts?

Therapist: It's one of the sections on the form between your automatic thoughts and your alternative thoughts!

Client: Oh, you mean the *thinking errors*.

Therapist: Yes! That's it! Now you said that the work had been useful up to the row, but then it's usefulness had been 'wiped out' by the row. Can you identify any thinking errors here?

Client: Well, I suppose I was overgeneralizing.

Therapist: Can you expand on that for me?

Client: Well, because we had a big row, and that was really dreadful, it doesn't mean that everything else going on for me has to be affected and it doesn't turn something that seemed helpful at the time into uselessness.

Therapist: How much do you believe that, Tom?

Client: Well, as I'm saying it to you now, I believe it a lot and it makes sense, but at the time, I just felt on a 'downer' and couldn't think of anything else except how dreadful it all was.

Therapist: Okay. Let me just feed that back to you. You said that when you had an argument with Kas, everything was 'wiped out'. Then looking back at the incident, you recognized that the row – although very disturbing to you at the time – didn't alter the usefulness of your new way of looking at your problems . . . If you had another similar row this week, do you think you would be able to view it in this new way?

Client: [*long pause while client looks away*] It's like I have two heads. There's the one I have as I sit here with you, and also as I'm filling out the forms, where I can look at things in a new light. But there's the one that's always been

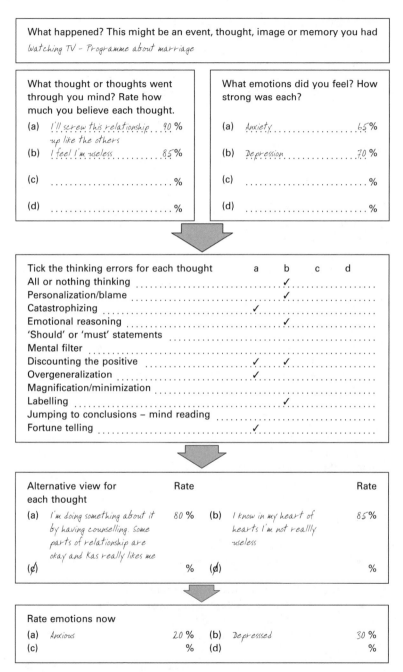

What happened? This might be an event, thought, image or memory you had

Watching TV - Programme about marriage

What thought or thoughts went through you mind? Rate how much you believe each thought.

(a) *I'll screw this relationship* 90 %
    up like the others
(b) *I feel I'm useless* 85 %
(c) .... %
(d) .... %

What emotions did you feel? How strong was each?

(a) *Anxiety* 65 %
(b) *Depression* 70 %
(c) .... %
(d) .... %

Tick the thinking errors for each thought   a   b   c   d

Thinking error	a	b	c	d
All or nothing thinking		✓		
Personalization/blame		✓		
Catastrophizing	✓			
Emotional reasoning	✓			
'Should' or 'must' statements				
Mental filter				
Discounting the positive	✓	✓		
Overgeneralization	✓			
Magnification/minimization				
Labelling		✓		
Jumping to conclusions – mind reading				
Fortune telling	✓			

Alternative view for each thought   Rate   Rate

(a) *I'm doing something about it* 80 % (b) *I know in my heart of* 85%
    by having counselling. Some   *hearts I'm not reallly*
    parts of relationship are   *useless*
    okay and Kas really likes me
(∅) .... % (∅) .... %

Rate emotions now
(a) *Anxious* 20 % (b) *Depresssed* 30 %
(c) .... % (d) .... %

Figure 2.7 *Automatic thought form*

> there, and can't bring in these new ways of thinking, when I'm right in the middle of a situation.
>
> *Therapist*: That's a very good point you've made. I think it is important for me to emphasize that we have only had a couple of sessions and that it will take time and practice to use the new skills you are developing in the *heat of the moment*. It is partly for this reason that I ask you to write out your difficulties and alternative responses on the forms so that you can gradually incorporate your new ways of thinking and feeling into your everyday life.

In this extract, the therapist and client continue to work through a typically structured session and proceed to discuss agenda items. The therapist assists the client to *examine and question unhelpful thinking (6)*, which includes identifying *thinking errors*. The therapist decided not to question the client's thinking errors of magnification or catastrophizing when he used the word 'dreadful' to describe an event. He made a mental note of this for later discussion and also led the client towards identifying and challenging a number of other thinking errors surrounding this one event. In this way, the therapist continues to socialize the client into cognitive behaviour therapy. This is aided by helping the client to recognize the importance of work outside of the sessions (see *8 Teach client to become own therapist*, p. 22) and also by helping the client to appreciate that it is unhelpful to view therapeutic change in all or nothing terms (see *thinking errors*, p. 12). The client's 'two heads' will only become one as he practises and assimilates new skills enabling him to bring new thinking patterns to current difficulties.

The present chapter has focused on the fundamental aspects of cognitive behaviour therapy and has concluded with annotated extracts which help to exemplify them while giving a flavour of cognitive behaviour therapy in practice. In the following chapters we consider the process in greater detail.

Practice points

1   Learn the cognitive model and use it daily in your own life to help you to understand it. Beliefs are learned and can be changed.

2   Use the ABC to help you to remember:
   - A = Activating event (event, image, thought, memory, etc.).
   - B = Belief (automatic thoughts and underlying beliefs).
   - C = Consequences (emotions, behaviour, physiology and further thoughts).

3   Recognize that thinking errors are central to the cognitive model: know them thoroughly.

4   Use basic counselling skills as a foundation for your practice of cognitive behaviour therapy.
5   Structure the therapy session by negotiating an agenda.
6   Familiarize yourself with the fundamental characteristics of cognitive behaviour therapy.
7   Remind yourself and your client of the importance the other 167 hours outside of the therapy session every week to put cognitive behaviour therapy into practice in the real world.

3

Assessment

'Assessment' is a very wide-ranging term which will be common to a broad variety of different practitioners, each having their own understanding, professional codes and practices and spectrum of application. For example, care managers/social workers, clinical and counselling psychologists, community mental health team members, community psychiatric nurses, counsellors, psychiatrists and psychotherapists will each have assessment tools pertaining to their area of work in mental health. There may be overlap within these various approaches to assessment and there are common elements to all of them (Palmer and McMahon, 1997). For the purpose of this book, we will focus on five main elements:

1 What is the problem?
2 Is cognitive behaviour therapy suitable for the problem?
3 Is the client suitable for brief cognitive behaviour therapy?
4 What are the thoughts underlying the problem: the cognitive conceptualization?
5 Transcultural and gender issues.

Although we have identified five separate elements, it is important to note that these are not separate but interrelated, as we shall demonstrate later. The reason for this is that we are basically assessing the fit of a therapeutic framework (cognitive behaviour therapy) against a client/problem (see Ruddell and Curwen, 1997). However, it will be useful initially to look at each of the elements separately. A further overriding aspect of assessment is that it is ongoing (as noted in Chapter 2) .

1 What is the problem?

Depending on the setting in which the cognitive behaviour therapist works, the client may or may not have already undergone an assessment in some form, varying in its thoroughness from client to client and from professional to professional. For example, a full mental state examination (MSE) may have been carried out (see Curwen, 1997; Lukas, 1993; Morrison, 1995) and a full diagnosis made adopting the classification system outlined in the fourth edition of the *Diagnostic and Statistical Manual of Mental Disorders* (DSM IV; American Psychiatric Association, 1994). Not all clients who seek counselling have had a mental disorder recognized and a number will not have a recognized disorder. For example, a person may simply lack assertion skills. However thorough or minimal an assessment has been, it is the task of the therapist to seek out the client's problem and to decide whether all or a part of it is amenable to cognitive behaviour therapy. For example, a person who presents with depression may also experience intense guilt. The therapist and client may be able to identify such a disturbing emotion and its associated thoughts, and by working through an emotional episode involving this emotion (examining and questioning unhelpful thinking) find a key to the client's wider emotional problems.

A helpful distinction can be made between mental disorders (as classified in the DSM IV) and the unhelpful negative emotions associated with these and perceived by the client. It is the latter of these with which the cognitive behaviour therapist, in collaboration with the client, predominantly works. In Chapter 2 we outlined the most common thinking errors identified in cognitive behaviour therapy. These thinking errors are summarized in Figure 3.1, where we have also attempted to identify specific thinking errors most common to particular unhelpful emotions. But it is important to note that these have not been identified through research and must at this stage be considered as no more than an informed opinion. The particular cluster of thinking errors for a specific unhelpful negative emotion will vary to some extent from client to client.

2 Is cognitive behaviour therapy suitable for the problem?

Beck's original work in cognitive therapy focused on depression (Beck, 1964). Attendance at current conferences finds cognitive therapists applying their approach to an ever wider range of problems such as relapse prevention in manic depressive psychosis, cognitive behaviour therapy of conduct-disordered children, cognitive behaviour therapy in recent onset acute psychosis and dialectical behaviour therapy as a treatment of borderline personality disorder. As a relatively young science/therapy, convincing outcome studies of treatments for the widest range of problems have yet to be produced, but some areas in which successful results have already been demonstrated are as follows:

- couples problems (Baucom et al., 1990)
- eating disorders (Agras et al., 1992; Fairburn et al., 1991; Garner et al., 1993)

	Anxiety panic, nervousness	Depression	Anger	Guilt	Hurt	Morbid jealousy	Shame/ embarrassment
All or nothing thinking	✓	✓	✓				✓
Personalization/blame		✓	✓				✓
Catastrophizing	✓	✓					✓
Emotional reasoning	✓	✓	✓	✓	✓	✓	
'Should' or 'must' statements	✓	✓		✓	✓	✓	
Mental filter		✓				✓	✓
Discounting the positive	✓	✓					
Overgeneralization	✓	✓	✓	✓			
Magnification/minimization	✓	✓			✓		
Labelling			✓				
Jumping to conclusions			✓		✓	✓	✓
(a) Mind reading	✓	✓					✓
(b) Fortune telling	✓	✓					✓

Figure 3.1   *Thinking errors for common problems*

Note: However, Blackburn and Eunson (1988) found that selective abstraction (mental filter) was most frequently associated with depressed mood while arbitrary inference (jumping to conclusions) was most frequently associated with anxious mood.

- generalized anxiety disorder (Butler et al., 1991)
- inpatient depression (Bowers, 1990; Miller et al., 1989; Thase et al., 1991)
- major depressive disorder (Dobson, 1989)
- panic disorder (Barlow et al., 1989)
- substance abuse (Woody et al., 1983)

These are areas in which evidence-based practice is now possible, although earlier in their evolution this would not have been the case. Obviously, at some point in time, all approaches to all problems would have been at the stage of hypothesis and not yet proven to be clinically effective through outcome research. Therefore cognitive behaviour therapy is currently being applied to a range of problems as the best approach at the present time, for a range of different reasons such as cost effectiveness, an alternative to prescribed drugs which may have unwelcome side-effects or addictive qualities, the ability to be used in group format, its relatively brief duration compared to other therapies such as psychoanalytic therapy and its user friendliness.

Once cognitive behaviour therapy has been applied to a problem type (such as panic disorder without agoraphobia) by a number of therapists practising with a range of clients, the most effective means of applying CBT to the problem may emerge. For example, therapy for panic disorder will include explaining to the client the cognitive model of panic outlined by Clark (1986, 1988) and this will be solidly embedded within the cognitive conceptualization of the client's problem, discussed later in this chapter. Even once a specific technique or more general approach has begun to be accepted within the helping professions of mental health, supported by some research, further research or meta-analyses may challenge high expectancies.

Two recent examples will illustrate this. First, brief psychological interventions (debriefing) for treating immediate trauma-related symptoms and preventing post-traumatic stress disorder have become popular, but a recent meta-analysis (Wessely et al., 1997: 1) concludes that 'there is no current evidence that psychological debriefing is a useful treatment for the prevention of post-traumatic stress disorder after traumatic incidents. Compulsory debriefing of victims of trauma should cease'. Second, a number of techniques called 'power therapies' (Figley, 1997) such as thought field therapy (TFT: Callahan, 1985), eye movement desensitization and reprocessing (EMDR: Shapiro, 1989, 1995), trauma incident reduction (TIR: Gerbode, 1988) and emotional freedom techniques (EFT: Craig, 1997) have been promoted as rapid cures for post-traumatic stress disorder, phobias, and an ever-widening array of clinical disorders.

However, a leading article (Rosen et al., 1998) suggests that they fare less well under controlled testing.

We shall shortly be considering the suitability of the client for brief cognitive behaviour therapy. One aspect which is important is whether or not the client has responded positively to the type of therapeutic work being offered. Similarly, where other indications and contra-indications are absent, the therapist can take a pragmatic stance from the outset. If the cognitive behaviour therapy approach seems to yield positive results quickly which are apparent both to the therapist and the client, this is a reasonable basis on which to continue.

3   Is the client suitable for brief cognitive behaviour therapy?

Ruddell and Curwen (1997), in considering brief therapy across a range of therapeutic orientations from psychodynamic to cognitive behavioural, have identified four main criteria from these varying protocols:

1   The person's problems are capable of clear identification, allowing a precise focus for therapy to be determined, and appear able to be sufficiently resolved within the brief time span.
2   The person has responded positively to the type of therapeutic work being offered either at first contact or during the initial session.
3   The person has sufficient understanding and motivation to work within the framework offered.
4   There are no major contraindications.

Safran and Segal (1990a) have developed the Suitability for Short-term Cognitive Therapy Rating Scale which can be used to assess clients formally by rating them from 0–5 on ten items, where a total of 0 indicates least and 50 indicates greatest suitability for short-term cognitive therapy. The items are given below with brief explanations. We use examples taken from our session with Tom in Chapter 2 as well as further examples in our first session with him to demonstrate how information gleaned from the client is used to support a particular score or rating for each of the ten items. Safran and Segal (1990b) have developed a short manual, *Suitability for Short-Term Cognitive Therapy Interview*. They suggest that the interview to decide on suitability of a client for short-term therapy should take approximately one hour and emphasize three important points. First, it is essential for the interviewer to have some basic biographical, historical and diagnostic information prior to the interview. Second, probes and

Items	Rating Scale (0–5)
1 Accessibility of automatic thoughts	
2 Awareness and differentiation of emotions	
3 Acceptance of personal responsibility for change	
4 Compatibility with cognitive rationale	
5 Alliance potential (in-session evidence)	
6 Alliance potential (out-of-session evidence)	
7 Chronicity versus acuteness	
8 Security operations	
9 Focality	
10 General optimism/pessimism about therapy	
	Total:

Figure 3.2   *Items in the Suitability for Short-term Cognitive Therapy Rating Scale*

successive probes are used to prompt the client 'to reveal whatever therapy-relevant capacities they have'. Third, the therapist is in no way bound to progress mechanically through the ten items in sequence, but is encouraged to move freely among them. Some probes may produce information relevant to more than one dimension (Figure 3.2).

1   Accessibility of automatic thoughts
Automatic thoughts were described in Chapter 2 (p. 9). This item is designed to assess the ability of the client to identify and report automatic thoughts once they have been described and exemplified by the therapist. In the first session with Tom, and with little prompting by the therapist, he was able to identify the automatic thought, 'I always make a mess of things'. We noted above that successive probes are given so that the clients have the best chance of revealing whatever therapy-relevant capacities they have. If Tom had not identified the automatic thought in this way the therapist would have prompted him further and further. For example, he may have asked Tom, 'What was going through your mind in the situation?' If this prompt failed he may have said to Tom, 'Can you picture yourself in that situation right now?', setting the scene further if necessary. If this prompt failed, the therapist might encourage Tom to focus on thoughts associated with emotions actually experienced during the session. In some heightened emotional experiences, especially where anger was involved, he had difficulty reporting his automatic thoughts and a score of 4 was therefore given for this item.

2   Awareness and differentiation of emotions

This item represents the ability of the client to access his emotions and to be able to distinguish between different emotions experienced. Tom had a good awareness of his emotions and was readily able to differentiate between feeling 'down', feeling 'guilty' and feeling 'angry'. It is important to emphasize that although a client may not use the same terminology as the therapist, such as 'low in mood' or 'depressed', this does not necessarily demonstrate an inability to differentiate between different emotions. On the contrary, although the therapist may socialize the client into the language of emotions commonly used in therapy, it is the responsibility of the therapist to check out the meanings of words and phrases used by the client. This is a particularly important issue in transcultural counselling (see Ruddell, 1997). A maximum score of 5 was given to Tom for this item.

3   Acceptance of personal responsibility

An important aspect of therapy is the extent to which a person recognizes his own part in creating the emotional difficulties he is experiencing. Following an early psychoeducational intervention, Tom noted, 'It was a relief to find out that I can do something about my problems . . . and that the way I think about things can make my problems worse, so if I start to think about things in a different way I could start to feel better.' Although Tom had some awareness and acceptance of personal responsibility for his own problems, he still attributed a considerable portion of them to external factors such as his partner. For this reason he was given a score of 3.

4   Compatibility with cognitive rationale

The cognitive rationale was outlined in Chapter 2 and the client's first introduction to it may be quite brief. Even at this point, clients vary enormously in the extent to which they recognize the connection between thoughts and feelings and, equally important, the crucial need for the client to work on his or her problems outside the therapy room by completing assignments at home. The previous extract also demonstrates that Tom recognizes the potential usefulness of the cognitive rationale. Although he experienced some difficulties in completing his homework assignment, he recognized the need for it and his failure to complete it was brought about not by his incompatibility with the rationale but by his unhelpful thinking patterns. His score for this item was 5.

5   Alliance potential in session

This item relates to the ability of the client to form a good working relationship with the therapist within the confines of the therapy room, an aspect we have discussed more fully in Chapter 2, where we also emphasized the important part played by the therapist in making this possible. In the first session with Tom it quickly became apparent to the therapist that he was prone to interpret some of the therapist's statements as personal criticism. It was largely the skill and openness of the therapist in exploring this in session that led to a greater alliance later on. Tom's score for this item was 3.5.

6   Alliance potential outside of the therapy room

This is an item designed to gauge the client's ability to form positive relationships in general. One of the main problems which led Tom into therapy was his difficulty in forming and maintaining close relationships; his thoughts surrounding this led him into depression. His relationship with Kas was erratic and these factors led to a low score of 2.

7   Chronicity of problems

The length of time over which a person has experienced problems is an important factor in deciding whether or not a particular client/ problem is suitable for brief cognitive behaviour therapy, but this is balanced against other dimensions on the rating scale. Another aspect of this item is that a person may have a problem of considerable duration for which brief cognitive behaviour therapy is not considered to be suitable, but may present with a further and discrete problem of more recent onset for which brief cognitive behaviour therapy may indeed be suitable. The previous entry noted that Tom's relationship difficulties were relatively chronic, but the recent episode of depression was of a lesser duration (approximately five months) which prompted a fairly high score on this item of 4.

8   Security operations

This item is a measure of the extent to which a client might engage in behaviours such as avoidances or excesses which preserve a sense of safety but which are nevertheless counterproductive to their well-being and to therapy. Tom was generally free from security operations with one major exception. He had developed a pattern of abandoning relationships when difficulties arose. The therapist believed there was a slim possibility that Tom may abandon therapy in a similar way if the therapeutic process became too difficult for him. A score of 4 was given for this item and the therapist made a mental note to be aware of such difficulties before they fully emerged so that positive action could be taken to prevent premature termination of therapy.

9   Focality
This is a measure of the client's ability to remain focused on the particular problem in hand. Tom was very able to concentrate on the central point being discussed, leading to a score of 5.

10   Client optimism/pessimism about therapy
The extent to which a client believes that a particular form of therapy will be effective in helping to resolve his or her problems is an important factor in deciding whether short-term therapy (and therapy in general) may be suitable. Tom scored highly again on this item (5) as he showed considerable optimism for cognitive behaviour therapy.

Tom scored a total of 40.5 on the Saffran and Segal Suitability for Short-term Therapy Rating Scale, which indicated that he was highly suitable for short-term cognitive behaviour therapy.

4   What are the thoughts underlying the problem: the cognitive conceptualization?

One of the main tasks of the cognitive behaviour therapist is to understand the client's problems in cognitive terms (Persons, 1989). This means recognizing the client's negative automatic thoughts (NATs) and the underlying unhelpful beliefs from which they emerge. The therapist identifies current thinking associated with and maintaining problematic behaviours, emotions, physiology and cognitions. We include imagery within cognitions, but it is useful to note that some practitioners prefer to regard imagery as a separate modality (e.g. Lazarus, 1981). Lazarus also searches for precipitating factors connected to the current problem and reinforcing the self-defeating unhelpful beliefs, and the client's unhelpful interpretation of major developmental events.

Cognitive behaviour therapy is distinguished from a number of other therapies such as psychoanalysis by focusing on the present and the very recent past. However, it acknowledges that unhelpful thinking is developed over time and therefore includes in the cognitive conceptualization of the client's problem the early development of unhelpful beliefs and the precipitation or activation of these underlying assumptions through one or more critical incidents. This cognitive conceptualization is shown in Figure 3.3. It is the key to the client's problem(s) and should be able forcefully and coherently to explain the breadth and depth of the client's difficulties. Coupled with empathy, the therapist will be able to use the cognitive

The past	The present
• Predisposing factors (early experiences):	• Maintaining factors (current situation):
assumptions and core beliefs formed	cognitions (negative automatic thoughts)
	emotions behaviour physiology
• Precipitating factors (critical incidents)	
intermediate and core beliefs activated	

Figure 3.3 *Components of cognitive conceptualization*

conceptualization to make sense of the client's problem and feel that if he, the therapist, was in the same life situation and experiencing the same thoughts and beliefs as the client, he, too would be experiencing emotional distress of similar type and magnitude. This is an important point for the brief therapist to grasp. The cognitive conceptualization may also be thought of as a map charting the client's emotional landscape and can be usefully disclosed to the client, when and if appropriate, as a psychoeducational aid encouraging insight and understanding.

We will consider Tom's difficulties as viewed through this cognitive conceptualization. Cognitive behaviour therapy focuses mainly on the present and recent past and it is here that we will begin to conceptualize Tom's problems. His letter of referral stated that he had been depressed for approximately five months and responded poorly to antidepressant medication. In Tom's *current situation* two main problems were apparent: depression and difficulty maintaining close relationships. Some of the *maintaining factors* present for Tom were as follows. His negative automatic thoughts commonly included overgeneralization and discounting the positive ('*everything got wiped out*'); all or nothing thinking ('I'm about to screw this relationship up'); personalization ('I'm useless – Kas is only asking for more commitment because she feels sorry for me'). These thoughts are consistent with the *cognitive triad* categorized by Beck (1967) who noted that the content of a depressed person's thinking is characterized by distorted negative thoughts about the *self*, the *future* and the *world* (Figure 3.4). Tom's *negative automatic thoughts* are

Figure 3.4   *Cognitive triad*

associated with other *maintaining factors*. His *mood* is low much of the time with periods of despair punctuated by anger, his *behaviour* is marked by inactivity, lack of motivation, tearfulness and explosive verbal outbursts followed by withdrawal and his main *physiological* difficulties are loss of appetite and disturbed sleep (early morning waking).

The main *precipitating factor* which led to the present episode of depression was that Kas wanted greater commitment from Tom. They had been partners for nearly two years and she wanted them to move in together. While this *critical incident* precipitated the recent onset of depression, it was preceded by an event in adolescence which precipitated the depression for the first time and involved Tom's then 'girlfriend' leaving him abruptly.

The *predisposing factors* most significant to Tom's current difficulties were that his mother was often absent from the home for long periods of time and his father was affectionless and over-critical although he provided for Tom's material needs (Figure 3.5).

5   Transcultural and gender issues

Issues about counselling across cultures and from one gender to another are important considerations throughout counselling and are not specific to brief therapy except that the time span imposes a further constraint on the development of the therapeutic relationship. We shall therefore not discuss this in detail except to highlight some of the major factors and to point the way to further work in this area. The main difficulties are understanding the client in his or her entirety, communication between client and counsellor (both verbal and non-verbal) and the imbalance of power within the counselling relationship.

We noted in Chapter 2 the basic elements identified by Truax and Carkhuff (1967) essential for the counsellor to incorporate into effective therapy. These are accurate empathy, being 'with' the client, understanding or grasping the client's meaning and communicating

Personal development	Cognitive development
Predisposing factors (early experience)	
Mother often absent	Assumptions and core beliefs
Affectionless and over-critical father	formed:
	'Something is wrong with me'
	'Nobody wants me'
	'I don't do anything right'
	'I'm not good enough'
Precipitating factors (critical incident)	*Intermediate and core beliefs activated*
Previous relationship abruptly ended (past)	Unknown at this stage
Greater commitment needed from Tom (recent past)	
Maintaining factors (current situation)	*Negative automatic thoughts*
Episode of depression	*Overgeneralization and discounting the positive:* 'Everything got wiped out'
Difficulty forming close relationships	
Emotions: Depression, anger	*All or nothing thinking:* 'I'm about to screw this relationship up'
Behaviour: Inactivity, lack of motivation, tearfulness, explosive outbursts and subsequent withdrawal	*Personalization:* 'I'm useless. Kas is only asking for more commitment because she feels sorry for me'
Physiology: Loss of appetite, disturbed sleep	

Figure 3.5 *Cognitive conceptualization chart (CCC) for Tom*

empathic understanding and unconditional positive regard. If a counsellor was unable to communicate effectively with a client, he would find it difficult to demonstrate any of these aspects. Communication usually implies a common language and common meaning system. If the cultures and gender of the counsellor and client are different, communication may be hampered to a greater or lesser extent. By acknowledging the client's right to be understood fully and recognizing that the probable power imbalance between counsellor and client is likely to be magnified across cultures, the effective counsellor will reach out to find a common framework for both cultures (Lonner and Sondberg, 1995). It is important for the counsellor to recognize that language difficulties will be a hindrance to effective communication and that other differences, including body language and diverse meaning systems across cultures (and gender is enculturated), present further challenges (see Palmer, 1999).

The brief therapist will therefore be particularly proactive but sensitive in seeking an awareness of cultural variations. In respecting the client she will be willing to accept that she has social and cultural biases of her own (see cultural empathy: Ridley, 1995). Ruddell (1997) has discussed particular difficulties in psychiatric assessment across cultures: Rack (1982), for example, has noted in considerable detail some of the problems involved in the mere recognition of disorders such as anxiety, depression, mania, schizophrenia, paranoia and hysteria in people who are not from white American or European cultures by someone who is. Signs and symptoms often have cultural specific meanings. The use of standardized psychometric instruments across cultures has been shown to be highly questionable (MacCarthy, 1998) and has contributed to some practitioners rejecting such assessment approaches (Parker et al., 1995).

In the present chapter we have focused on aspects of assessment from a brief therapy perspective and have endeavoured to indicate areas where brief cognitive behaviour therapy might be the therapy of choice for particular clients/problems. Where it is not appropriate for a particular client/problem, this does not mean that cognitive behaviour therapy is unsuitable and the same practitioner may be able to consider such therapy. However, where the therapy which the counsellor has to offer is not suitable for the presenting client/problem (for example, where cultural differences are too great for the therapist to understand the client's problem, or where the client remains completely unconvinced that the therapy could be helpful) the therapist will need to consider referring the client on to other sources of help (Ruddell and Curwen, 1997). Assessment in the wider context is more fully discussed in *Client Assessment* (Palmer and McMahon, 1997).

Practice points

1   Establish main client problem(s) and develop tentative cognitive conceptualization but recognize that assessment is ongoing.
2   Recognize the thoughts underlying the client's problems, including the main thinking errors.
3   Decide whether brief cognitive behaviour therapy is appropriate for the client and her problem(s) at the present time.
4   Use our four-point criteria (in 'Is client suitable for brief cognitive behaviour therapy?') and the Safran and Segal Suitability for Short-term Cognitive Therapy Rating Scale to inform the above decision.

5 Decide with other professionals such as psychiatrists, general practitioners, etc. whether brief cognitive behaviour therapy is to be used alone or in conjunction with other therapies, such as chemotherapy (see Chapter 1).

6 Recognize that assessment, diagnosis and the use of psychometric instruments across cultures presents special problems.

7 Accept that you have cultural and social biases of your own.

8 Be aware that power imbalances already existing between client and counsellor are magnified across cultures.

9 Be proactive but sensitive in seeking an awareness of your client's culture: acknowledge your client's right to be understood.

10 Recognize that your assumptions and practices are not absolute and reach out to find a framework of meaning common to the cultures of your client and yourself.

4

Beginning Stage of Therapy

Therapy may begin within the assessment phase depending on the type and extent of the client's problems. This is common in brief therapy. We noted in Chapter 2 that brief cognitive behaviour therapy is goal directed and that the client's goals for therapy are collaboratively decided upon. In this and the following two chapters we will demonstrate that the therapist also has goals to meet in order to enable therapy to be optimally effective. These goals change over the course of therapy and can be broadly divided into three phases: beginning, middle and end. They will be firmly held in the therapist's mind and will strongly shape the course of therapy. However, we also noted that a key tool in brief cognitive behaviour therapy is the cognitive conceptualization of the client's problem(s). The brief cognitive behaviour therapist holds the therapist goals and the cognitive conceptualization in tandem. Together, they largely determine the course of therapy in harmony with the fundamental characteristics of cognitive behaviour therapy outlined in the 'whistlestop tour' of Chapter 2.

The first part of this chapter will therefore outline and explore these goals. We will then suggest how they might be integrated into the first therapy session, the structure of which is unique and therefore different from the typical session format outlined in Chapter 2. We will introduce a number of common client problems within the chapter and give some indication of what might be achieved within the beginning phase of therapy.

Therapist's goals

Beginning stage of therapy

Identified in Figure 4.1 are therapist goals common to the beginning stage of brief cognitive behaviour therapy. The brief cognitive behaviour therapist can use this as a checklist between sessions to help keep the therapy strongly focused. Although the items in the list are ordered, with items at the top of the list generally having precedence over those at the bottom, we do not suggest that the order be slavishly adhered to. In discussing the suitability for short-term

1   Develop cognitive conceptualization of client's problem(s).
2   Develop and maintain collaborative therapeutic relationship.
3   Educate client about his or her disorder and help to alleviate client distress through psychoeducation.
4   Help client to distinguish between different emotions.
5   Teach the cognitive model.
6   Help the client to identify his or her automatic thoughts.
7   Help the client to link automatic thoughts with emotions and behaviours.
8   Help the client to recognize that he or she is responsible for personal change.
9   (Begin) to help the client examine and question his or her automatic thoughts and to develop more helpful alternatives.
10 Help the client develop optimism about cognitive behaviour therapy.
11 Elicit doubts about therapy and help client to alter any misconceptions through psychoeducation.
12 Discover what the client wishes to achieve through therapy and collaboratively agree realistic client goals (focality).
13 Security operations: establish the extent to which the client engages in behaviours that temporarily relieve and/or enable avoidance of the problem but which are countertherapeutic.

Figure 4.1   *Checklist of therapist's goals: beginning stage of therapy*

therapy rating scales (Safran and Segal, 1990a,b) in Chapter 3, we noted that two or more items might be covered within a single section of dialogue. Similarly, two or more therapist goals might be achieved in parallel. For example, in helping the client to develop optimism about brief cognitive behaviour therapy, the therapist might also be developing and maintaining a collaborative therapeutic relationship. Although the checklist at first appears to be lengthy, a number of the elements can easily be subsumed under a much shorter list of headings once the trainee therapist has fully understood and integrated these into his or her practice. After discussing and demonstrating the elements of this checklist, the shortened version will be presented.

1   Develop cognitive conceptualization of client's problem
This chapter commenced with an indication that the cognitive conceptualization was a primary factor guiding the course of therapy. It is almost impossible to emphasize this strongly enough. Although the conceptualization may develop over time, the lack of a firm formulation is often one of the major factors in preventing therapy from being as brief as possible. The conceptualization itself has been more

fully discussed in Chapter 3. We recommend that it be introduced to the client at an early stage of therapy when appropriate so that the client can assess how well it seems to fit her problem. It is useful to write the formulation on a whiteboard during the therapy session. Where the client disagrees with the formulation, or does not seem to find it adequate, the reasons are best openly discussed and the formulation altered as necessary. The whiteboard allows for alterations to be made with ease. The client may not seem to find the conceptualization to be a convincing and powerful explanation of his or her problems even though it appears from open discussion to have no major inaccuracies. In such a case the client may not fully believe that cognitive behaviour therapy will be helpful for his or her problems. This is an aspect which would hopefully have been recognized at the assessment for brief therapy stage (but is also discussed at item 11 of this checklist).

2   Develop and maintain collaborative therapeutic relationship

Item 3 of the fundamental characteristics of cognitive behaviour therapy in Chapter 2 has already discussed this important aspect of therapy. Establishment of such a relationship is essential to successful therapy and is analogous to preparing the ground from which good growth can take place. As noted previously, the therapeutic relationship is collaborative in cognitive behaviour therapy in general and in brief cognitive behaviour therapy in particular. A fine balance is required between maintaining this relationship and enabling a range of cognitive behaviour therapy techniques to be brought into therapy at an appropriate pace. A similar balance should be found between maintaining the collaborative relationship and keeping interventions both brief and clinically relevant. In brief therapy everything the therapist says is intended to be optimally therapeutic, whether this be eliciting, examining or questioning the validity of a negative automatic thought, distinguishing between emotions or alleviating the client's distress. In many cases, a single word will lead the client forward in the session without the need for extended dialogue from the therapist (see verbal economy in Chapter 7). The therapist gives positive feedback at every opportunity for even the smallest progress made by the client. We have also noted that the cognitive behaviour therapist adopts a *directive* therapeutic style. However, the hallmark of a good therapist is that this style operates through the collaborative relationship and does not deteriorate into an autocratic or authoritarian process. Brief cognitive behaviour therapy is more successful when it is founded on a two-way relationship, with therapist and client working together to tackle problems.

A simple example of this process might be helpful. Emmelkamp (1994) has reviewed treatments for specific phobias and the research suggests that where the fears are specific and circumscribed brief in vivo exposure treatment is effective. However, if the therapist pushed ahead with this against the will of the client, for example, exposing the client with arachnophobia to large spiders without appropriate preparation and support, treatment is likely to be ineffective.

3   Educate client about his or her disorder and help to alleviate client distress through psychoeducation

We emphasized in Chapter 2 that cognitive behaviour therapy is psychoeducational, mainly focusing on psychoeducation as the means by which the cognitive model together with the process of change is conveyed to the client. In this section the focus is on educating the client about his or her disorder, especially where the client's thoughts and beliefs about the disorder lead to considerable distress. Ellis (1962) has noted that we often disturb ourselves about our disturbances. For example, a person may be anxious about being anxious, or thinking that their anxiety problem leads to the loss of some part of their life; a person may become depressed about being anxious. Many combinations are evident: guilt about being depressed; shame about being depressed; anger at being depressed or anxious; shame about being jealous – the list is endless. In addition to these second order emotions about primary problems, third or fourth level emotions or beyond may be generated, such as depression about anger being anxious. Dryden (1995) refers to these as *meta-emotional problems* and suggests that it is beneficial to work with these prior to the primary emotional problem if the meta-emotional problem interferes with therapeutic work in the session or home assignments outside of the session; where the meta-emotional problem has escalated to the extent that it has become clinically more important than the primary problem or where the client believes it would be beneficial to address the meta-emotional problem first. (Also see metacognitions, Wells, 1995, 1997.)

When a client shows distress about his or her problem or disorder, it is helpful to explore this and provide explanations as appropriate. In many instances, simple information at this stage may be all that is necessary to alleviate the secondary distress and free the client suffi-ciently to work on the primary problem. For example, a sales manager required publicly to demonstrate his figures to the board of directors found it increasingly difficult to concentrate on this task and experienced angry outbursts which were becoming more frequent. He concluded that he was 'cracking up'. He was relieved to discover this was not a sign of impending madness but a symptom of being extremely overworked, leading to stress coupled with performance anxiety.

Where a person's problems clearly involve a known psychiatric disorder, as classified by the American Psychiatric Association (1994) or World Health Organization (1992), bibliotherapy (Lazarus, 1971) may be helpful in dispelling unfounded myths and beliefs and informing him or her about the condition, while providing useful information about self-help (Ruddell and Curwen, 1997). The major categories of psychiatric disorder are summarized in Appendix 12 (also see Curwen, 1997). Materials used range from simple information leaflets such as those produced by professional bodies about single disorders, for example, anxiety, depression, obsessive-compulsive disorder or schizophrenia, etc., to fully developed self-help manuals (Greenberger and Padesky, 1995).

4   Help client to distinguish between different emotions

In Chapter 3 the suitability of a client for short-term cognitive behaviour therapy was discussed and one of the items in the Safran and Segal scale was the ability to distinguish between different emotions. This is important in brief cognitive behaviour therapy for a number of reasons. We have noted elsewhere that thoughts and feelings occur together. It follows that the type of thought a person has is consistent with the type of feeling they experience. For example, if a person has the thought 'I'm useless and I hate myself', she is unlikely to feel happy at that moment! It is therefore important in cognitive behaviour therapy for therapist and client to be able to distinguish clearly between different emotions. The consistency between particular thoughts and particular emotions is also useful for enabling the therapist to check parts of the cognitive formulation. For example, if the client presents with depression, but the automatic thoughts elicited early on in therapy are ones which are consistent with anxiety (agoraphobia), such as, 'if I go to the shops I just know I'll faint', then the depression may be a secondary emotion based on further thoughts such as, 'I'll always be like this; I'll never be able to go out on my own again' (see item 3 of these goals).

Some clients are able to distinguish between thoughts and emotions and between different emotions with relative ease while others have varying degrees of difficulty. Where clients use the terms thoughts and feelings almost interchangeably, it may be useful to say to him something such as: 'I noticed just now when I asked you what *thoughts* went through your mind that you described how you were *feeling*. It is important in our work that we are able to separate out the thoughts from the feelings so that we can understand more fully how they are linked together.' For clients who have not practised distinguishing between thoughts and feelings, a suggestion such as this may be all that is necessary, with further short prompts as appropriate (see item 6 for examples).

Some people have difficulty in separating and identifying different feelings and this is not surprising because a person with meta-emotional problems (see item 3) may have several emotions linked together in close succession and experience them as a single negative experience. This is usually quite easily picked up by the therapist because expressions used are vague and indistinctive, such as 'I felt really shitty', 'I felt dreadful', 'I was bad', and so on. A helpful way to assist the client is to take the adjective he has used and ask, 'Did you feel shitty *anxious*, shitty *depressed*, shitty *angry* or something else?' A technique used by Albert Ellis is to ask the client to take a wild guess at the emotion. It is important for the therapist not to assume that the client is being vague about an emotion when he is simply being idiosyncratic or using language differently to the therapist. This is particularly important when working transculturally. Similarly, individuals may have come to associate a feeling with something which represents it.

5 Teach the cognitive model

The cognitive model was discussed in Chapter 2 and the shortform, ABC, was introduced as a useful mnemonic device. In practice, some clients seem to grasp this shortform almost immediately while for others it seems to obscure the learning process. This may be because the word 'activating' is not particularly memorable or commonly associated with the word 'event' in most people's minds, while the word 'belief' is not commonly associated with 'automatic thought' in most clients' minds and the connection between automatic thoughts and beliefs is often not grasped until a little later in therapy. Since home assignments are a central part of therapy, repetition through the use of automatic thought forms (see Chapter 2) is often a more effective means of learning the event–thought–consequences chain.

The first introduction to the client of the cognitive model is best achieved through taking a particular emotional event which the client freely introduces and eliciting the thoughts and feelings associated with it. For example, if a client is experiencing low mood a recent occasion can be asked for and discussed. The therapist takes every opportunity to reinforce the cognitive model, particularly in the early stages of therapy, by consistently helping the client to link thoughts with consequences (see second and third items listed below). This linking is both explicit ('let's see what thoughts you were able to identify in the automatic thought form you did for last week's assignment') and implicit ('so the thought "I will make a fool of myself" led you to feel anxious').

The following are the main components to be covered in explaining the cognitive model to the client. They are not in the order in which they would be presented to the client:

- The 'event'.
- Thoughts and beliefs.
- Consequences: emotions or feelings, behaviours, physiology.
- Alternative thoughts and beliefs.
- Change.
- Thinking errors.

THE 'EVENT'   This is often an 'event' in the client's life and may be large or small. It is often unfavourable in the client's view, such as 'Maria didn't turn up' or 'I'd just had another storming row with Johnathan', but by no means always. In fact, the 'event' may be *anything which the client can get upset about*, whether or not he or she recognizes it at the time or understands why. In practice it is sometimes necessary to infer backwards from the negative emotion to discover what the 'event' is. For example, the client may explain that he was in the kitchen preparing tea and for no apparent reason 'came over all sad'. It is not uncommon for the event to be a thought and meta-emotional problems discussed above are an example of this. Other 'events' which are not observable in the external world are sensations such as daydreams or images (particularly common in post-traumatic stress disorder, PTSD), voices (especially in schizophrenia), bodily sensations (common in anxiety or somatic disorders), smells and others. It is preferable for the therapist not to go into too much detail in the early stages of therapy.

THOUGHTS AND BELIEFS   Thoughts and beliefs were discussed in Chapter 2. In teaching the cognitive model to the client, the main concept to be demonstrated is that *emotions are mediated by thoughts*. Where a client has been able to generate an event and is aware of the automatic thought preceding a negative emotion (see next section), the following type of questioning may help to demonstrate that thoughts influence emotions.

> Therapist: You said that when you felt sad this morning, you had the thought, 'I always make a mess of everything'. You also said that you'd completed a report at work that you were quite pleased with. How, then, does it follow that you make a mess of everything?
> Client: [*after a pause*] Well, I guess it doesn't really.

> Therapist: If you had said to yourself this morning that you mess some things up, but only some things and not everything, do you think you would have felt the same?
>
> Client: I'd have felt sad, but nothing like the way I did this morning.

This connection between thoughts and feelings can be worked with further in the session. We noted earlier that more than one of the therapist's goals (for the beginning stage of therapy) may be worked upon simultaneously. In the above extract, the therapist was not only demonstrating the link between thoughts and feelings, but was already starting to examine and question the client's unhelpful automatic thoughts. Where an alternative to the negative automatic thought is not readily generated, a more direct approach may be attempted:

> Therapist: If, instead of the thought [*insert client's automatic thought*] you had the thought [*suggest an alternative to the unhelpful thought*], how do you think you would have felt then?

Where this fails, the following sometimes succeeds:

> Therapist: Can you think of a friend who might have experienced the same event but felt differently?
>
> Client: Yes, Daniel.
>
> Therapist: What do you think he might have been thinking to lead him to feel that way?

It is generally helpful to illustrate these examples using the ABC model on a whiteboard during the therapy session to reinforce the B–C connection.

CONSEQUENCES (OF HOLDING PARTICULAR BELIEF)   In demonstrating this part of the model, the main concept to convey to the client is that *immediate consequences usually ensue from an automatic thought (or belief)*. If the therapist has been successful in demonstrating the role of thoughts in the last section, some of the consequences of holding particular thoughts will already be apparent to the client. It will then only be necessary to help the client to discover that there are other consequences such as behaviours and bodily reactions.

> Therapist: Jane, you said that when your employees 'act casually' you feel really angry. Can you tell me if you have noticed any changes in your body when this happens? . . .
>
> [*Jane gives examples*]
>
> Therapist: And do you find yourself doing anything different when this happens?

ALTERNATIVE THOUGHTS AND BELIFS   When teaching the cognitive model, the main purpose is not to attempt to change the client's thoughts or beliefs (although as we demonstrated above this may already begin to occur), but to demonstrate that alternative (and more helpful) thoughts and beliefs are possible. It is preferable to help the client to generate these alternatives him or herself.

CHANGE   Many clients are quickly able to understand the parts of the model discussed so far. However, a large number say that although they can understand the model intellectually, they are far less certain about its ability to bring about positive change to their problem situation. This is particularly apparent with people who say that they experience some of the counter-negative thoughts (or helpful alternatives) at the time the 'event' is taking place. The reader will also note that the extent to which the client believes cognitive behaviour therapy will be useful in overcoming his or her problems is one of the items on the suitability for short-term cognitive therapy rating scale. It is important to convey to clients that change comes about through practice and that maintaining good mental health is accomplished by doing (rather than through insight alone), in just the same way as physical health needs to be maintained. Hence the need for assignments between sessions. Additionally, Ley (1979) has demonstrated that people commonly retain only a small proportion of information provided to them in consultations. One goal of between-session assignments is to aid the recollection of information: the cognitive model itself, alternative (more realistic) beliefs generated by the client in the session and psychoeducational material.

Because of the difficulty clients often experience in recalling material from the session, they are routinely encouraged to keep a therapy notebook to record salient points during the session. Many also find it helpful to audiotape the session so that relevant parts can be played outside the session to aid understanding. It is also important to acknowledge that we are commonly indoctrinated into holding unhelpful negative thoughts and beliefs through our early socialization process and beyond: change may take time. Often, by carefully exploring an emotional episode in session and discovering more helpful responses together, an otherwise sceptical client will recognize the gentle power of this approach.

It is also important to note that cognitive behaviour therapy is aimed at helping people to change their emotional problems, not to overcome practical problems (Bard, 1980). Poor housing conditions, low income, illness, unemployment and impending divorce are common examples. Yet cognitive behaviour therapy may be appropriate where the client has developed an emotional problem of which this practical problem is the focus (Ruddell and Curwen, 1997). It may also give the client the emotional space to deal more effectively with his or her practical problems (Ellis, 1985). Additionally, where the focus on automatic thoughts reveals that the thoughts do not particularly involve thinking errors, problem solving could be the most effective intervention (see Hawton and Kirk, 1989; Meichenbaum, 1985; Milner and Palmer, 1998; Palmer, 1994; Palmer and Burton, 1996; Wasik, 1984).

THINKING ERRORS   The most common thinking errors (or cognitive distortions) have been outlined in Chapter 2. At the stage of teaching the client the cognitive model, the main points to convey are that *we often adopt (learn) thoughts or beliefs that are unhelpful to us* and that *these thoughts and beliefs are not supported by objective evidence*, although they may seem true, plausible and believable to the client at the time; *new thoughts or beliefs can be learned or adopted*. It is not necessary at this stage to cover all the thinking errors in detail as these can be scrutinized by the client as an assignment outside therapy and linked to the automatic thought forms. It is only necessary to demonstrate to the client the way in which thinking errors can lead to unhelpful negative emotions.

6   Help the client to identify his or her automatic thoughts
The ease with which a client is able to identify his or her automatic thoughts is one of the items in the suitability for short-term cognitive therapy rating scale discussed in Chapter 3. As the detection and identification of such automatic thoughts are central to cognitive behaviour therapy, it is important for the therapist to have a number of techniques available to help a client develop the skill necessary to become aware of and identify these negative automatic thoughts early on in therapy. A helpful distinction for the therapist to keep in mind is between the ability of the client to identify the thoughts going through his or her mind in association with a negative emotional episode and the recognition of such thoughts as being negative automatic thoughts. Many people who come into therapy recognize the thoughts they have, but do not recognize that they are negative or unhelpful. Where this is so, it is often sufficient to bring this to the client's attention. Then the therapist focuses on the identification of such negative thoughts in session and this is continued as an external assignment, using automatic thought forms (see Chapter 2). Many clients, however, are not aware of the thoughts they have running through their minds in association with negative emotions, but can quickly learn to detect them through prompts in the session such as, 'what was going through your mind at that point?' or 'what were you *telling* yourself when that happened?'

We noted in section 4 that Ellis encourages clients to 'take a wild guess' if they find difficulty identifying an emotion. Similarly, clients can be asked to take a wild guess at what automatic thought(s) they had in a particular situation if these are not apparent. This is the basis of Burns' 'stick' technique, but in pictorial form (Burns, 1989). He encourages people to draw an unhappy 'stick' figure when unable to identify negative automatic thoughts and to draw a 'thought bubble' over the stick figure's head, as in a cartoon; then to fill in the thoughts the 'stick figure' is having.

A further method is to ask the client what another person, such as a good friend, might be thinking if he was experiencing the same emotion(s) in the same situation. As the therapist will have generated a cognitive formulation of the client's problem(s), she can guess the automatic thought (where other approaches have failed to yield it) and ask the client if the thought seems to fit. When using approaches such as these, it is important to check out with the client that the thought(s) generated are indeed fitting.

Sometimes the reason that a person is unable to report an automatic thought is that in the therapy room she is too far removed from the situation to be able to recall her 'hot cognitions'. One way to aid the client is to help her to reconstruct the troubling situation in her mind by encouraging her to focus on it in detail. She may be asked fully to describe the environment in which it occurred while paying attention to what she was doing at the time and what she was experiencing in each of her senses. Further feelings may arise with associated thoughts which the client may now be able to access. A vivid image is sometimes most prominent and the client can be asked, 'did any images flash through your mind at the time?'

Where the client is still unable to recall automatic thoughts associated with a disturbing event, it may be helpful for the therapist to use material from an 'event' actually taking place in the therapy session. The therapist closely follows the client's mood and when a negative shift is perceived asks, 'I thought you suddenly looked sad when we were just talking . . . can I check this out with you?' The client affirms this. 'What was going through your mind at that point?' Checking out whether the client was sad (or anxious, angry, guilty, etc.) can be left out by an experienced therapist, by simply asking 'What was going through your mind just then?' However, this may challenge the therapeutic relationship if the client believes that the therapist is telling the client how she feels (emotional rape), or if it seems to the client that the therapist is engaging in distorted thinking – mind reading!

Where an 'event' is an interaction, a further technique is for the client and therapist to role play the situation and for the therapist to ask at the appropriate point, 'What was going through your mind just then?' As automatic thoughts are usually evaluative, another way to discover such a thought is to ask, 'What did that situation *mean* to you?'

Finally, if all these approaches fail, a technique based on para-doxical intervention may be attempted. Here, the therapist suggests a thought which seems to be the opposite of what he believes the automatic thought to be (Beck, 1995):

> Therapist: Are you telling yourself that you would like to do well but it does not really matter if you don't?
>
> Client [interrupts]: No! I must do well otherwise it would prove I'm a failure.

We noted above that the cognitive formulation helps to guide the therapist as to the accuracy of an automatic thought. Where a feeling and a reported automatic thought do not seem to fit, this may be because the automatic thought is associated with a meta-emotional problem. It follows from this that if a client reports an automatic thought it is helpful to check whether any other automatic thoughts are evident as they may relate to meta-emotional problems, which in some circumstances are best tackled first. When to do so is discussed above.

Where all attempts by the therapist fail to elicit automatic thoughts in a range of situations and experiences reported by the client, the therapist may wish to reassess whether or not the client is really suitable for brief cognitive behaviour therapy. In some cases, it may be possible to proceed by working more behaviourally. How-ever, in endeavouring to elicit the client's automatic thoughts it is important not to suggest through over-zealousness that the client has failed in some way. If the therapist picks up from the client's changed body language that she may be feeling this, it will be beneficial to raise the issue with her. This may in itself be an episode generating hot cognitions, which can be used as material for further therapeutic work in the session.

Where it seems impossible to discover the client's automatic thoughts, it is worth remembering that the client may be experiencing a meta-emotion about experiencing the original emotional episode in the first place (e.g. shame about feeling anxious), or about his inability to access the automatic thought now. If this seems to be so, the therapist can say to the client, 'Many people feel ashamed at feeling the way they do and sometimes think they are alone in the way they feel – I wonder if you are having such feelings?' Some clients who do not report automatic thoughts may be holding a belief such as, 'This is all a waste of my time – why doesn't she do something more constructive to help me.' Again, the therapist can check out with the client whether or not she believes this type of therapy may be effective for her and routinely ask how the client found the session to be at its end.

7   Help the client to link automatic thoughts with emotions and behaviours

The linking of thoughts with emotions and behaviours has already been discussed in the previous section. Thoughts will also be linked to a person's physiological responses. The main purpose of this item is to encourage the client to practise the identification of their thoughts and the link to their emotions, behaviours and bodily sensations *over and over each time they are experienced outside of the therapy room.* The client comes to recognize that whenever unpleasant emotions are experienced, so are the associated automatic thoughts. By doing this in association with the automatic thought forms, the client can quickly be led to discover that he often uses a small group of the thinking errors in many situations.

8   Help the client to recognize that he or she is responsible for personal change

Helping the client to recognize that he or she is responsible for personal change is made easier if therapeutic goals are clearly and collaboratively identified and if the cognitive formulation of the client's problems is well formed. The cognitive formulation will include elements that recognize the extent to which the client's present difficulties (and negative automatic thoughts) were firmly founded on a socialization process which enabled them to develop. For example, if a significant other constantly told the client as a child 'you're a dunce – you'll never amount to anything', it would be easy to appreciate that the client may have developed low self-esteem. Once the client understands the cognitive model, can identify negative automatic thoughts and recognizes some of the thinking errors he brings to his current situations, while being aware of therapeutic goals, he is in a better position to be able to change. While the client may not actively seem to choose to adopt his negative automatic thoughts, he implicitly does so if he does not question their validity by looking for the evidence supporting them. However, considerable effort may be required by the client if they have practised thinking errors over many years.

We emphasized the importance of between-session assignments or homework in Chapter 2. Such work is important in cognitive behaviour therapy in general (Niemeyer and Feixas, 1990; Persons et al., 1988) and crucial in allowing brief therapy to be brief. However, doing such work between sessions may be problematic for some clients at any stage of therapy and a discussion of approaches to dealing with this is included in the next chapter. We also noted the benefit of the client keeping a therapy notebook to record important points during the session.

9   *(Begin) to help the client examine and question his or her*
     automatic thoughts and to develop more helpful
     alternatives

This process is first started in the therapy room. Usually a client is asked for a problem, and the automatic thoughts are elicited by the therapist (see sections 6 and 7). The therapist usually adopts a questioning style, sometimes known as socratic questioning or socratic style rather than direct disputation or indoctrination, whereby the client is led inexorably towards challenging his own beliefs (Beck et al., 1979). This process often leads to cognitive and emotive dissonance.

In the following extract, the client (who is coming towards the end of the beginning stage of therapy) is describing a problem at work where he needs to pass a number of people from another department in the confined space of a corridor. An automatic thought form is used (see p. 12 and Appendix 2).

Client: They may have caught my eye and expected me to say hello or something and then I would have felt anxious.

Therapist: What was anxiety provoking in your mind about the situation?

Client: When I'm in a situation where I have to speak I get all hot and bothered and sometimes I just freeze up.

Therapist: What thoughts come into your mind when you think of that situation?

Client: If I freeze up they will think I'm stupid and a waste of time to talk to.

Therapist: On our scale of 0–100, how strongly do you rate your belief in that thought?

Client: About 85.

Therapist: Going back to your thought about people thinking you're stupid, what follows that in your mind?

Client: That makes me useless and I'll be left all alone with no friends.

Therapist: You said you felt anxiety in this situation. Do you feel any other emotions?

Client: Yes. I feel depressed too.

Therapist: Can you rate each of those emotions?

Client: Hmm. Anxiety 80 per cent and depression about 70 per cent.

Therapist: Let's return to your first thought. Have you frozen up in this way, recently?

Client: Yes. A couple of weeks ago, it happened to me at a party.

Therapist: Can you think of any situations where you've been with people and not frozen up?

Client: I am talking to you okay I suppose . . . and there's also Annie at work who I can talk to . . . I've got three good friends who I feel relaxed with.

Therapist: Do these five people think you're stupid?

Client: I don't think so . . . It's just that when I'm with people I don't know, I can't think of anything interesting to say.

Therapist: Are you ever quiet with the three good friends you feel relaxed with?

Client: Sometimes, I suppose.

Therapist: And do you think they see you as stupid?

Client: No. No, I don't think so.

Therapist: If the people in the corridor spoke to you, and you did freeze up, is there anything else they might be thinking about you other than that you're stupid?

Client: Hmm . . . I suppose they might possibly think I'm shy, or maybe aloof, or preoccupied with something or just in a quiet mood.

Therapist: How would you rate your belief in each of these?

Client: Shy: 75 . . . aloof: 50 . . . preoccupied: 65 . . . quiet mood: 70.

Therapist: So if you take all of those possibilities, and I'm sure we can both think of many others, how strongly do you now rate your belief in your original thought that these people will think you're stupid?

Client: It's much lower. About 35 or 30.

Therapist: And how are you feeling now?

Client: Much less anxious . . .

Therapist: Can you rate that for me please?

Client: About 25 or 30.

This extract relates to a person who experiences social phobia. In practice, the therapist would also encourage the client to engage in a number of behavioural tasks. He may also use psychoeducation aimed at conveying to the client that the freezing up he experiences is common to this type of problem and may go into some detail to explain the way in which such anxiety leads to the client's reduced ability to interact socially.

10   Help the client develop optimism about cognitive behaviour therapy

and

11   Elicit doubts about therapy and help client to alter any misconceptions through psychoeducation

The extent to which a client is optimistic about cognitive behaviour therapy is one of the items on the suitability for short-term cognitive therapy rating scale which we introduced in Chapter 3. Material for these two items will arise throughout the therapeutic session, but may be most common when teaching the cognitive model, when helping the client to examine and question his unhelpful thoughts and when asking for feedback at the end of each session. As indicated in Chapter 2, any misconceptions about cognitive behaviour therapy are openly discussed through socratic dialogue (see 9 above) whereby the client is led to question his own misconceptions and through this process the therapeutic alliance is deepened. These items are also closely related to the extent to which the client accepts responsibility for personal change. However, although such responsibility ultimately rests with the client, the therapist is responsible for helping the client to find the means by which such change may come about. Although the therapist wishes to develop client optimism, he is nevertheless realistic and conveys to the client that therapy may not be a straight progression but one where ups and downs sometimes occur.

*12   Discover what client wishes to achieve through therapy
and collaboratively agree realistic client goals
(focality)*

This item has been discussed in Chapters 2 and 3. The clearer the goals, the greater will be the ease with which focality may be maintained. We have discussed elsewhere that clients will often express goals which are rather vague and need to be collaboratively clarified. Also common is the expression of a long-term goal which needs to be broken down into small manageable and achievable steps. If these steps, or sub-goals, are to be achieved, they may in turn require the client to carry out a number of tasks and behavioural experiments. Tasks are generally assignments designed to help the client to engage in previously avoided situations. Experiments are assignments that help clients to check out the validity of their negative automatic thoughts which may lead to a shift in their unhelpful beliefs. It is important to grade such work sufficiently so that each task and experiment is challenging but not overwhelming (see Palmer and Dryden, 1995). Below are some of the goals, sub-goals, tasks and experiments which were agreed with the client we met in section 9 above.

- *Goal*: ask woman out for a date.
- *Sub-goal*: interact in social settings without too much anxiety.
- *Task*: to enter a number of specified social situations – local pub, work canteen, badminton evening class, phone old acquaintances.
- *Experiment*: ask strangers to change money while smiling at them (to check out belief that they will be unfriendly).

*13   Security operations: establish the extent to which the
client engages in behaviours which temporarily relieve
and/or enable avoidance of the problem but are
countertherapeutic*

These behaviours may be very wide ranging and present themselves in many different forms, from avoiding eye contact to excessive alcohol consumption. The avoidance is of the anxiety-provoking event and, as discussed above, an event may be a thought. Thoughts may include images or memories. Avoidances may be active or passive (Kirk, 1989). Active avoidances are things which have been started as a means of coping with the problem, such as the development of specific rituals in obsessive compulsive disorder. Passive avoidances are things which have been stopped, in an attempt to help with the problem, such as not going to the shops in agoraphobia. Some questions which may be helpful in eliciting these security operations are as follows.

1   *Active*:
    'If the problem went away what could you stop doing?'
    'Have you started doing anything new, or started doing things differently, because of the problem?'
2   *Passive*:
    'Have you stopped doing things or stopped going to any places because of the problem?'

We have now discussed the checklist of therapist's goals for the beginning stage of therapy in some detail and will shortly present their integration into the first therapy session. We started the chapter suggesting that these goals could be subsumed under a shorter list of headings once the trainee therapist has fully understood and integrated these into his or her practice. These are now suggested in Figure 4.2, which also acts as a reminder of the items from the original list subsumed under each of the main headings.

First therapy session

The structure of the first therapy session is different from subsequent sessions mainly because the client has not yet been introduced, and socialized into the process of cognitive behaviour therapy. For example, the client may not be aware of the cognitive model and will therefore require an introduction to it in the first session. The structure of the first session is outlined in Figure 4.3. The assessment interview for brief cognitive behaviour therapy may have included a limited introduction to the cognitive model, usually the link between thoughts and feelings. In the dialogue below, we will give an example of the way in which the process of brief cognitive behaviour therapy is introduced to the client, but we will not present the whole of the interview as a number of the items have already been covered in the text above.

The following extract is taken from a first therapy session. The dialogue will be interrupted with a commentary in which the items

Collaborative relationship
2 Develop and maintain collaborative therapeutic relationship.
3 Educate client about his or her disorder and help to alleviate client distress through psychoeducation.
10 Help the client develop optimism about cognitive behaviour therapy.
11 Elicit doubts about therapy and help client to alter any misconceptions through psychoeducation.
12 Discover what client wishes to achieve through therapy and collaboratively agree realistic client goals (focality).

Cognitive model process
1 Develop cognitive conceptualization of client's problem(s).
4 Help client to distinguish between different emotions.
5 Teach the cognitive model.
6 Help the client to identify his or her automatic thoughts.
7 Help the client to link automatic thoughts with emotions and behaviours.

Help client to work on problem(s) in and out of session
8 Help the client to recognize that he or she is responsible for personal change.
9 (Begin) to help the client to examine and question his or her automatic thoughts and to develop more helpful alternatives.
13 Security operations: establish the extent to which the client engages in behaviours which temporarily relieve and/or enable avoidance of the problem but are countertherapeutic.

Figure 4.2 *Therapist's goals: a framework for the beginning stage of therapy*

1 Set agenda.
2 Check client's mood.
3 Review presenting problems which emerged at evaluation for brief therapy interview, identify current problems and agree client goals.
4 Outline cognitive model.
5 Review client's expectations of therapy.
6 Psychoeducation about client's particular disorder.
7 Agree between-session assignment(s).
8 Summarize session.
9 Obtain feedback on session.

Figure 4.3 *Structure of first therapy session*

above are demonstrated. The therapist and client have already greeted each other.

> *Therapist*: I'd like to begin this session by introducing you to agenda setting. This is where we can decide upon what we'll talk about today. It is helpful to do this at the start of each subsequent session and we do this in order to cover the most important issues. I have some items to suggest go on the agenda and there will be opportunity for you to add anything more. How's that?
>
> *Client*: Okay.
>
> *Therapist*: We will need to get to know each other a little better and in this first session we have a lot of ground to cover. This will make this session slightly different from later ones. I'd like to check out how your mood has been and also what it was that brought you to brief cognitive behaviour therapy. It is important for me to know what some of your problems and difficulties are and what you wish to accomplish and expect from therapy. Is that okay?
>
> *Client*: Yeah okay.

In these few brief sentences, the therapist has introduced the concept of therapy following an agreed agenda and has already suggested some of the initial items. He continues to develop the agenda with the client. In future sessions the therapist will encourage the client to take ever greater responsibility for setting the agenda where possible. It is not uncommon for the experienced therapist to digress from the agenda if the course of the session dictates this: for example, later in therapy, in the agenda item, it becomes apparent to the therapist that the client has not understood a salient point, which has prevented him doing his between-session assignment (the next agenda item). The therapist and client therefore agree to allocate the item sufficient time on the present agenda.

> *Therapist*: I'll write these on the agenda for today. [*The therapist uses a whiteboard, leaving gaps for further items to be added.*] I'd also like to explain how this therapy will go and find out from you what you may already know about brief cognitive behaviour therapy. We'll discuss what you might attempt between sessions and towards the end I'll summarize the main points for today and ask you for feedback on how you thought the session went . . . Would you like to add anything else to the agenda at this point?
>
> *Client*: I don't think so.
>
> *Therapist*: Now that we've agreed today's agenda I'd just like to check out how your mood has been this week before moving on to look at your problem in depth. Can I see the questionnaires which you have filled out? [*Client hands over the forms and therapist scans through them.*] Since the assessment session there seems to be some change in your mood. Can you tell me how you've been feeling?
>
> *Client*: I'm glad I've made the choice to do something about my problems but feel slightly worse overall, especially at work. I still feel depressed, tired all the time and lethargic.

Therapist: Hmm. Would it be helpful to add to the agenda some information about how depression commonly affects people in ways other than mood.
Client: Yes. Yes, it would.

Agenda setting is an important aspect for any trainee therapist to learn. Failure to do so may hinder both therapist and client from focusing on relevant and important issues. The actual setting of the agenda is swift and to the point but allows for active and structured client participation. An explanation of the rationale enables the client easily to understand the process of therapy and he or she will learn how to contribute to the agenda.

In this first session the therapist next does a brief mood check. Questionnaires such as the Beck Depression Inventory (BDI: Beck, 1978), the Hamilton Rating Scale for Depression (HRSD: Hamilton, 1960), the Beck Anxiety Inventory (BAI: Beck and Steer, 1990), the Hamilton Anxiety Scale (HAS: Hamilton, 1959) and the Beck Hopelessness Scale (Beck et al., 1974b), together with the client's and therapists' subjective observations, enable both objectively to evaluate the client's progress. Thorough examination of these questionnaires may also highlight problems not reported verbally by the client, for example, feelings of guilt, suicidal ideation, difficulties sleeping and reduced sexual drive (Curwen, 1997; McMahon, 1997; Ruddell, 1997).

If these objective tests are unavailable or the client is unwilling or unable to complete the forms (possibly due to difficulties with reading or writing), the therapist has the option of teaching the client how to rate his or her mood on a 0–100 scale, 0 representing no depression (or other emotion) and 100 representing the worst. (See item 9 of *Therapist's goals*, p. 57.) However, the reason for the client's unwillingness to complete the forms is best openly discussed as it may be that the thought of completing them constitutes an 'activating event' which will be suitable material for examination through the cognitive model. It is essential to assess for hopelessness and suicidal thoughts during the initial session and establish the seriousness of such thoughts. The therapist is advised to ask questions and gather more information on whether or not plans have been made, how well developed these plans may be and what prevents the person carrying out such an action. For more information on suicide see Curwen (1997) and Chapter 9.

The next extract of dialogue illustrates how the therapist may review the presenting problems which emerged at the assessment for brief therapy interview and proceeds to identify current difficulties.

Therapist: When we met at the assessment session, you said that you had been feeling depressed for at least two months, you had stopped socializing with friends and were becoming withdrawn. Have I got this right?

Client: Yes that's right.

Therapist: Have there been any major changes to your situation since then?

Client: Well, as I mentioned earlier, I'm finding it hard to cope at work as I'm so tired and lethargic all the time.

Therapist: What do you see as your main difficulties at the present time?

Client: This feeling of depression and work are getting me down. I've just been promoted and I'm under a lot more pressure. I'm not sure I'm up to the new post. I feel so tired and lethargic. Even getting up in the morning is an effort. I just don't know what's happening to me.

Therapist: It all sounds very difficult for you. If we were able to break this down into more manageable pieces it might feel less overwhelming. It seems that there are three aspects to your difficulties at the moment. One is that you're feeling pressurized in your new post. The second is that you're feeling so tired and lethargic and the third is about dealing with your feelings of depression.

Education about the client's disorder, in this case depression, has already been placed on the agenda (item 6). The therapist proceeds to link and explain the behavioural and physiological components of depression (problems at work, tiredness and lethargy) with others that are troubling the client. The therapist and client continue from the above extract to develop goals for therapy following the recommendations in item 12 of the therapist's goals (p. 59).

In the next extract, the therapist introduces the cognitive model (after establishing that the client has no knowledge of cognitive behaviour therapy other than that gleaned at the assessment interview for brief cognitive behaviour therapy). The model is usually introduced to the client using material from the client's recent past. Before proceeding, you may wish to refresh your memory of the model as outlined in Chapter 2 and as discussed in items 4, 5, 6, 7 and 9 of the therapist's goals. In the first session, the intention is not to provide a comprehensive and exhaustive account of the model, but sufficient for the client to recognize, experientially, that thoughts influence feelings and that thoughts are accessible to change.

Therapist: Jan, I'd like to explore the way in which your thoughts affect how you feel. Can you recall a time over the last week when you've noticed a down-turn in your mood?

Client: Hmm . . . Yes. I was at work and one of the men came back late from lunch. [*Activating event*]

Therapist: . . . and what emotion did you feel?

Client: I felt down . . . depressed. [*Emotional consequence*]

Therapist: Can you remember what was going through your mind?

Client: Well, I was thinking, 'I should have said something to him about being late but I'm just not up to it.' [*Beliefs*]

Therapist: That's a really good start. Identifying and evaluating thoughts is something we'll be doing a lot more of later and a skill which needs to be practised, like any other skill. So now, can we go back to your thoughts and

check them out? You had two thoughts, 'I should have said something' and
'I'm just not up to it'?

Client: Yes. That's right.

Therapist: And these thoughts, 'I should have said something' and 'I'm just not
up to it', led you to feel a wave of depression?

Client: Yeah.

The therapist writes this example on the whiteboard under ABC (as
described in Chapter 2). She proceeds by asking the client for a
further couple of examples where she has noticed her mood worsen
and helps her to elicit the thoughts associated with this.

Therapist: With these examples in mind, can you tell me about the connection
between thoughts and feelings?

Client: Well, it looks like what I think leads to changes in the way I feel.

It is important for the client to come to the conclusion that her
thoughts influence her feelings rather than the therapist telling her
this. The focus on several examples helps to reinforce her understanding. This is further consolidated by bibliotherapy and the
gathering of further examples by the client between sessions. Within
the session, the therapist continues by starting the process of gently
challenging the client's unhelpful thinking (for example, see item 9 of
the therapist's goals).

Throughout therapy the therapist makes capsule summaries.
During the early stages of the first therapy session this will be with
the aim of communicating understanding and giving full attention to
what the client has said. This aids the development of the therapeutic
relationship. Summaries are also beneficial in giving feedback to the
client that her difficulties have been taken at face value and that the
therapist has a sufficient understanding of the main problem areas.
As therapy progresses it is helpful for the therapist to encourage the
client to summarize the main points discussed in each session. This is
aided by the client's use of the *therapy notebook* to record important
points during the session. The end of session summary in this first
therapy session aims to pull together all the main points discussed (as
in the agenda), strengthen the client's understanding and review what
tasks the client has agreed to do between sessions. Where possible,
the therapist uses the client's own words in any forms of summary,
but it is important to note that in the final summary he does not
activate negative thoughts distressing to the client (Beck, 1995).
Feedback from the client is asked for and is the final item on the
agenda. This provides an opportunity for the client and therapist to
discuss any misunderstandings or misconceptions which are relevant
to therapy (for example, see item 11 in therapist's goals). In this final
extract the therapist summarizes at the end of the first session.

Therapist: Jan, we have now covered all of the items on our agenda and now I would like to summarize the main points that we have discussed today. Okay?

Client: Yeah.

Therapist: Well, we started with setting the agenda, which is how we will start all our future sessions. We then moved on to check out how your mood has been and looked at your current difficulties. You were able to set yourself some realistic goals for therapy which we will work on in future sessions. We discussed the use of the cognitive model as a way of helping with your difficulties, looking at how your thoughts affect how you feel. You noted that 'how you think leads to changes in the way you feel'. We have also explored the many ways in which having depression can affect you. As we worked our way through today's agenda there were some points which you wrote down to work on in preparation for our next session. Do you think these tasks are achievable for you?

Client: I think so.

Practice points

1   Use the cognitive conceptualization and therapist's goals to guide the course of therapy.
2   Know the therapist's goals well and use as a checklist between sessions.
3   Remain focused within the session by using the shortened framework of therapist's goals:
    - collaborative relationship
    - cognitive model process
    - help client to engage fully in working with his problems.
4   Use the guidelines for structure of the therapy sessions and note the altered structure of the first therapy session.

5

Middle Stage of Therapy

The focus of therapy shifts over its course. We noted in Chapter 2 that the separate *fundamental characteristics of cognitive behaviour therapy* merge into each other and in Chapter 4 that the therapist's goals are significantly interdependent. Similarly, the beginning, middle and end stages of therapy overlap considerably, but it is particularly important for the brief therapist to acknowledge the changing focus of therapy over time. This recognizes that therapy, however brief, is a developmental process. As a developmental process, its course and speed are determined partly by the client, his problems and resources, as well as the expertise and experience of the therapist. The focus of therapy shifts over its course, but consistency is aided by the cognitive conceptualization discussed in Chapter 3. The cognitive conceptualization remains central throughout therapy but may itself be built upon and modified as new psychological material emerges to support or nullify initial tentative hypotheses. As noted in Chapter 4, the brief cognitive behaviour therapist holds the cognitive conceptualization and the therapist's goals in tandem as they largely determine the course of therapy in harmony with the fundamental characteristics of cognitive behaviour therapy outlined in the 'whistlestop tour' of Chapter 2.

In the previous chapter we presented the therapist's goals for the beginning stage of therapy in some detail and this was shown in summary as Figure 4.1. Figure 4.2 subsumed all of the therapist's individual goals under three important and overarching themes:

1   Collaborative therapeutic relationship.
2   The cognitive model process.
3   Help the client to work on problem(s) in and out of therapy.

As discussed in Chapter 4, these three areas form the structure of therapy, and the goals the content. In this and the next chapter, you will find that the structure contained in (1) to (3) above remains the same, while the content (the goals) changes to reflect the development of the therapeutic process. These goals will shortly be presented to you within this framework, but it is important to recognize that some of the existing goals may continue to require attention or need to be revisited. For example, the process of therapy may have pro-

1   *Collaborative therapeutic relationship*
(a)   Continue to maintain collaborative therapeutic relationship.
(b)   Continue to give positive feedback and encouragement.

2   *The cognitive model process*
(a)   Shift focus of therapy from negative automatic thoughts to
       intermediate and core beliefs (as necessary).
(b)   Educate client about self-acceptance (as necessary).

3   *Help the client to work on problem(s) in and out of therapy*
(a)   Pass responsibility for therapeutic work over to client.
(b)   Encourage client to become own therapist.
(c)   Encourage client to continue with tasks between sessions.
(d)   Prepare client for setbacks and ending therapy – lapse or relapse
       reduction.

Figure 5.1   *Therapist's goals: middle stage of therapy*

gressed satisfactorily, but during feedback in one of the sessions in
the middle stage of therapy, client doubts about therapy emerge (see
item 11 of Figure 4.1). Here, the therapist will temporarily revert
back to an earlier goal and proceed as discussed previously in
Chapter 4. Figure 5.1 outlines the therapist's goals for the middle
stage of therapy.

The remainder of this chapter will focus on the individual items
presented in Figure 5.1. We will systematically discuss each of the
items in the above order although these are not sequential in practice,
but co-exist. For example, you may at a particular point in therapy
be educating the client about self-acceptance (2b), preparing the
client for setbacks (3d), while giving positive feedback and encouragement (1b) and continuing to maintain a collaborative therapeutic
relationship (1a)

1   Collaborative therapeutic relationship

(a)   *Continue to maintain collaborative therapeutic relationship*

We have discussed the importance of the collaborative therapeutic
relationship (also known as the therapeutic alliance) in previous
chapters and will not discuss it further here. Its importance does not
wane as therapy progresses and its development is central to overcoming difficulties which will almost surely emerge over the course of
therapy.

(b)   Give positive feedback and encouragement
Feedback is a term originating from systems theory. In brief cognitive behaviour therapy (and other forms of therapy) feedback is
information given to the client to let him know that he is on track.
This is done regularly and in a variety of ways. It is important to note
that feedback is given for even very small movement made by the
client towards therapeutic goals. This conveys to the client that he is
progressing in therapy and helps both to move therapy along and to
develop client optimism. Where setbacks occur, these are best viewed
in a wider context as troughs in an overall progressive process, with
emphasis on the gains which have been attained so far. The following
extract gives an example of feedback being given.

> *Therapist*: How did you get on with the thought forms you took away to do for
> your assignment?
> *Client*: Well, I found it easy enough to put down what happened, how I felt and
> the thoughts that ran through my mind, but I had some problems in
> believing very strongly in alternatives.
> *Therapist*: Just identifying those three steps is a really good start which many
> people don't latch on to straight away.

2   The cognitive model process

*(a)   Shift focus of therapy from negative automatic
thoughts to intermediate and core beliefs (as
necessary)*
Brief cognitive behaviour therapy aims to bring about the minimal
change necessary to enable the individual to carry on with her life
effectively. In practice, this means helping the client to return to a
point where she can continue to reach short- and long-term goals
*consistent with her ability to do so prior to the difficulties which
brought her for therapy*. If she requires long and deep work such as
addressing characterological problems (e.g. axis II problems as
defined in DSM-IV, i.e. personality disorders) brief therapy would
not be chosen (Freeman and Jackson, 1998).

For some clients, work at the negative automatic thought level
may be all that is necessary to improve functioning and lessen
emotional distress for the client to be satisfied that he has achieved
his goals. A number of people will continue to experience an abund-
ance of negative automatic thoughts driven by their underlying
(intermediate and core) beliefs. For this group of people, work at
this deeper level will be necessary. Regardless of whether or not you
and the client proceed to work on his underlying beliefs, the brief

cognitive behaviour therapy process usually commences with identifying and modifying automatic thoughts. Automatic thoughts are more accessible and more easily modified than underlying beliefs (which generate the thoughts and images forming the content of the automatic thoughts). This is consistent with schema theory discussed in Chapter 2. Therapeutic work on identifying and modifying automatic thoughts is usually necessary before effective therapeutic work is possible on underlying beliefs. However, it is worth noting that in schema focused therapy the core beliefs are tackled at an early stage of therapy. The majority of this chapter will outline the process of working with underlying beliefs and look at a range of techniques required to accomplish it. Before doing so it is important that the therapist is clear about the differences between automatic thoughts, intermediate beliefs and core beliefs.

To summarize, automatic thoughts represent the stream of thoughts, ideas and images which constantly accompany an individual as he or she proceeds through normal daily life. Negative automatic thoughts are those images and ideas which usually give rise to unhelpful negative emotions such as anxiety or depression. They are generally accepted as plausible and true by the client initially, but are not supported by objective evidence. They have been discussed previously along with the common 'thinking errors' or 'cognitive distortions' which they contain, such as overgeneralization, discounting the positive or mind reading. It is important to note that negative automatic thoughts arise in normal experience – they are not an abnormal activity. The cognitive model proposes that we distort incoming information to fit pre-existing conceptual frameworks in order to make sense of the world and our experience. Research supports the view that this is part of 'normal' experience (Hollon and Kris, 1984; Nisbett and Ross, 1980). When a person is emotionally distressed, the proportion of negative automatic thoughts increases. This is understandable because these thoughts arise from underlying beliefs. Underlying beliefs are of two main types: core beliefs and intermediate beliefs. As their name suggests, core beliefs are the foundations upon which other beliefs are built. They enable us to describe ourselves, others and the world in very general terms and are therefore 'overgeneralized, inflexible, imperative and resistant to change' (Beck et al., 1990b: 29). They are 'part of normal everyday processing of information' (p.32) and may be positive ('I am worthwhile', 'others are trustworthy' or 'the world is safe') or negative ('I am unlovable', 'others are aggressive' or 'the world is dangerous').

The other type of underlying beliefs are called intermediate beliefs because they exist between core beliefs and automatic thoughts. Like core beliefs, they are often unarticulated. Intermediate beliefs can be

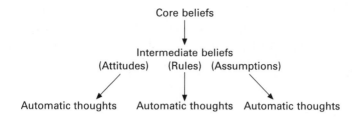

Figure 5.2 *The structure of beliefs: schema representation*

divided into three types: attitudes, rules and assumptions. We will explain later in the chapter why it is helpful to do so. Attitudes are evaluative, 'it's terrible to be unlovable', rules demanding, 'I must be loved' and assumptions conditional, 'if I am unlovable, then I am worthless'. (See Figure 5.2.)

The next part of this chapter will be divided into two sections: A and B. Section A will outline eight interventions used to discover and identify underlying (intermediate and core) beliefs. Section B will consider a range of techniques for modifying these beliefs once uncovered.

A IDENTIFYING UNDERLYING (INTERMEDIATE AND CORE) BELIEFS

As explained above, two types of belief underlie automatic thoughts: core beliefs and intermediate beliefs. Generally, in the same way that automatic thoughts are usually more easily accessed than the two types of underlying belief, intermediate beliefs are usually more easily accessed than core beliefs. This is understandable in view of the structure of schemas outlined in Chapter 2, where automatic thoughts are nearest the surface of consciousness and core beliefs are buried most deeply. The following section outlines eight methods the therapist commonly uses to help the client to identify underlying beliefs.

1 Underlying belief as automatic thought
We noted above that underlying beliefs are further from the surface of consciousness than automatic thoughts. This is generally so, but there are exceptions when clients express underlying beliefs as automatic thoughts. This happens by chance rather than resulting from a method, but requires the vigilance and knowledge of the therapist to *recognize an underlying belief stated as an automatic thought*. To the extent that they arise involuntarily in this way, the expression of underlying beliefs as automatic thoughts may seem to present the

erapist with an easy means of working at a deeper level. However
lution is needed, because clients who express such beliefs may not
yet be suitably prepared to work with them if insufficient work has
been achieved in identifying and modifying automatic thoughts. If
this is the case, the therapist will retain the underlying belief for
future work so as not to overwhelm the client by working at too deep
a level prematurely.

> *Therapist*: . . . and what thoughts went through your mind at that point?
> *Client*: I can't cope with this workload. It's all pointless. *I'm incompetent and
> inadequate.*

When clients express underlying beliefs as automatic thoughts early
in therapy, they are not usually aware of any difference or particular
significance as they have not yet progressed into that stage of the
cognitive model.

2   The downward arrow technique

This is a very popular technique devised by Burns (1980) and is also
known as the *vertical arrow technique* (Burns, 1989). The therapist
first identifies an automatic thought. Instead of attempting to modify
the thought in one of the ways we have outlined in the previous
chapter, the therapist temporarily remains with the thought by
asking the client, 'Suppose that was true, what would that mean to
you?' This type of questioning is continued until one or more
underlying beliefs are reached. Other similar questions may be used
such as: 'What would that say about you?'; 'What would happen
then?'; 'If so, what would be so bad about that?' (Fennell, 1989). An
intermediate belief is most likely to be elicited by asking what a
thought means to the client and a core belief most readily accessed by
asking what a thought means about the client (Beck, 1995).

In the previous chapter, we noted that some automatic thoughts
may be more pertinent to the client's emotional difficulties than
others. To maximize brevity, techniques such as this are best suited
to automatic thoughts which seem most strongly related to the
client's main problems (consistent with the cognitive conceptualization). Padesky (1994) consistently asks clients what a particular
thought says about (a) self, (b) others, and (c) the world, because a
person's emotions, behaviours and motivations are influenced by the
interactions of these three types of belief. It is important when using
this technique to recognize the belief once it is expressed. This is
sometime quite obvious, for example, 'I'm worthless', 'I'm a failure',
'I am helpless', but not always. When the client expresses a core
belief in his personal language (see section B) it may be less obvious.
Some examples are, 'I am a "hollow man"', 'I'm 2.4' and 'I'm a

Dodo'. Some indications that an underlying belief has been arrived at are a noticeable shift in mood at the expression of the statement, such as tearfulness, changes in facial expression or body language, or the same belief is said in different ways or even repeated. The downward arrow technique used to elicit underlying beliefs is demonstrated in the extract below in which we once again meet Tom.

- *A* Situation: argument with Kas.
- *B* Automatic thought: 'what's the point of carrying on with this relationship?'
- *C* Emotions: depressed and angry.

> *Therapist*: Suppose it were true that there is no point carrying on with this relationship. What would it mean to you?
> *Tom*: I'm going to screw up another relationship.
> *Therapist*: Suppose you did? What would it mean to you?
> *Tom*: That I don't do anything right.
> *Therapist*: And suppose you don't do anything right. What would that mean to you?
> *Tom*: Something must be wrong with me.
> *Therapist*: And suppose it is? What then?
> *Tom*: I'm not good enough.
> *Therapist*: What does that mean, 'not good enough'?
> *Tom*: Nobody will want me . . . I'm unlovable.

3 Suggest a theme linking various automatic thoughts
Beck et al. (1979: 247) outline the general process of identifying underlying beliefs as having three stages:

- Client recognizes and reports automatic thoughts.
- General themes are abstracted from these thoughts.
- Central rules or equations which the client holds about his life are delineated or formulated.

> *Therapist*: Tom, it's important in our work to look out for common themes which link a number of different problem areas for you. I've been listening carefully to the thoughts you've been having and I'm picking up a theme which seems to be something like, 'I must be loved'. Does that seem to fit?

4 Ask the client for a theme linking various events
We have already noted that therapeutic work does not usually begin to focus on underlying beliefs until the client has gained some skill in recognizing and modifying automatic thoughts. In considering the automatic thoughts which have emerged across a range of situations, the client can sometimes be prompted to reveal an underlying belief which seems to be pertinent for a number of them.

> *Therapist*: Tom, you've done some really good work both here and in your assignments on finding and challenging your automatic negative thoughts in quite a few different types of situation. Can you see any common theme in all of this?
> *Client*: Well, I guess I'm wanting to be loved.

The therapist can use these various methods either singly or together. For example, he can bring in sentence completion at this point to focus a little more clearly:

> *Therapist*: Staying with that theme, how would you complete the sentence, 'I am _____.'
> *Client*: I am . . . unlovable.

Asking the client for a theme linking a number of automatic thoughts across different situations will not work successfully for a number of clients such as those who have done little work on automatic thoughts, those with little 'insight' and those who are prone to wander off tangentially. Where this is so, one of the other methods will be preferable.

5   Ask client directly for belief

This intervention is a very direct way to elicit underlying beliefs and is suitable for only a limited number of clients. The caution noted in item (1) is applicable here too. However, some people are able to identify an underlying belief if simply asked to do so. Where such a question elicits other material, it is preferable to move on to one of the other techniques described in this section. We have said that work at this level is preceded by identification and modification of automatic thoughts. The therapist will only use this intervention if reasonably sure that the client is both ready (based on previous therapeutic work) and able (having regard for his ability to understand and conceptualize problems) to work in this way.

> *Therapist*: What is your belief about screwing up another relationship, Tom?
> *Tom*: I've screwed up so many, I must be unlovable.

6   Sentence completion

This is a relatively straightforward method in which clients are asked to complete a simple series of sentences preferably with a single word. Padesky (1994) gives the following examples. 'I am _____', 'People are _____' and 'The world is _____'. Tom completed the sentences in the following way: 'I am unlovable.' 'People are critical.' 'The world is aggressive.'

7 Provide first part of assumption

In Chapter 2 intermediate beliefs were shown to be composed of attitudes, rules and assumptions. Assumptions can usually be seen to have two parts: if _____, then _____. For example, 'if I am nice, then people will like me.' Beck (1995) uses a form of sentence completion by supplying the first part of an assumption and asking the client to complete the second part.

> *Therapist:* Tom, you started with the thought, 'what's the point of carrying on this relationship'. If there's no point carrying on this relationship, then what?
> *Tom:* Then it proves that nobody wants me . . . that I'm unlovable.

8 Belief questionnaires

In Chapter 2 we noted that a range of clinical measures such as rapid assessment instruments (or questionnaires) are available to the cognitive behaviour therapist. A number of belief questionnaires are available for the client to complete which can then be collaboratively considered with the client to establish her most central underlying beliefs. Examples of belief questionnaires are the dysfunctional attitude scale (DAS) (Weissman and Beck, 1978; Weissman 1979, 1980), the schema checklist (Beck et al., 1990a) and the schema questionnaire (Young, 1992).

Psychoeducation about underlying beliefs

After the therapist has identified one or more underlying beliefs, some preparatory psychoeducational work will be necessary to give the client a framework from which to understand the role of such beliefs. The rationale need not be extensive and depends on the individual's mental and emotional characteristics. As indicated elsewhere, this work will continue to be guided by the (evolving) cognitive conceptualization, the therapist's goals for therapy and the fundamental characteristics of cognitive behaviour therapy.

> *Therapist:* Tom, we've now arrived at a stage in therapy where we are beginning to identify what your underlying beliefs are. If you recall we spoke about these underlying beliefs loosely much earlier in therapy. This belief 'I'm unlovable' is what we call an underlying belief. Have you any idea where this comes from?
> *Tom:* It seems to stem from my childhood. I didn't feel loved as a child.
> *Therapist:* So if your parents had shown you love, would you have felt differently now?
> *Tom:* Oh definitely.
> *Therapist:* That seems to suggest that these beliefs you have that 'I'm unlovable' have been learned by you. Does that seem to follow?
> *Tom:* Yes. Yes, I can see that.

Therapist: So you learned the belief 'I'm unlovable'. People used to think the world was flat, but we now have a more realistic belief that the world is round, based on evidence. You too can learn more realistic beliefs and our work will focus on some methods to help you to do this.

Tom: That's good, but it all seems so difficult.

Therapist: At times when you are not depressed this belief 'I'm unlovable' probably does not affect you so much and is less strongly believed. However, when particular life events, such as rejection, activate your belief, 'I'm unloveable', you become depressed.

Tom: I think so.

Therapist: In addition, once you become depressed any evidence that contradicts this belief is passed over and discounted. Evidence which supports this belief is seized upon and you allow it to enter into your mind which proves to you how unlovable you are. In a sense you allow in the negative evidence and filter out the evidence which contradicts your belief. Does this seem to fit what you are doing?

Tom: Yeah. That seems to follow.

In the above extract the therapist has shown to the client that unhelpful underlying beliefs are learned. They may originate from early life experiences but are not necessarily true. They are maintained through faulty information processing. Being learned, they can be tested and found to be based on insufficient evidence. New beliefs are therefore possible.

B   MODIFYING UNDERLYING (INTERMEDIATE AND CORE) BELIEFS

Before we consider individual interventions which can be used for modifying underlying beliefs, some general guidelines will be suggested. Automatic thoughts are generally more transitory, while underlying beliefs are relatively resistant to change. Therapeutic work on modifying underlying beliefs develops from the process started with automatic thoughts and several important elements are applicable to work with both.

First, the process of encouraging the client to discover more adaptive alternatives to negative automatic thoughts is an important one. It demonstrates that automatic thoughts are learned. They can therefore be unlearned or more adaptive thoughts learnt in their place. This is a concept which is applicable to underlying beliefs and important to convey to the client prior to the process of modifying these deeper beliefs (see p. 78).

Second, we noted that it is preferable to summarize and give feedback to the client using her own words. This is equally important when working with underlying beliefs, because of the special meanings which particular words or phrases may convey to an individual. If the therapist paraphrases a client's belief, its meaning to the client may be altered or in some cases entirely lost. The wider the difference between the cultures of client and therapist, the greater the probability that the meaning will be lost in interpretation. Once core beliefs have been identified it is important to name or label them, using the client's own personal language. Padesky (1994: 269) notes that doing so brings about greater affect from the client associated with the schema and resulting change is more deeply held. She recommends the following type of questioning: 'How would you say this in your own words?' 'Can you give me an example of how this works in your life?' 'Do any images or memories come to mind associated with this belief?'

Third, we noted that therapist and client do not scrutinize all negative automatic thoughts, but only those which are central (consistent with the cognitive conceptualization) or otherwise important (such as those with high affect). Underlying beliefs are treated similarly. Because more work and effort is generally required to bring about change to an underlying belief, such focus is particularly important. This will be more apparent in using some interventions than in others. For example, use of the dysfunctional attitude scale (DAS) developed by Weissman (1980) may indicate that the client holds a number of dysfunctional beliefs drawn from seven main categories: approval, love, achievement, perfectionism, entitlement, omnipotence and autonomy. The scale itself will indicate which unhelpful beliefs are held most strongly. These can be agreed with the client aided by the cognitive conceptualization. Using his own words they can then be personalized and modified.

Fourth, if a client is to move from the position of believing strongly in an unhelpful underlying belief, he will find it very difficult to do so unless there exists a more helpful alternative to believe in. This is a little different to work with automatic thoughts, which because they are generally more transitory, less rigid and global can usually be more easily weakened or dislodged. Helpful beliefs are also referred to as positive, adaptive, functional, rational, realistic or problem, solution, task and goal focused, while unhelpful beliefs are negative, maladaptive, dysfunctional, irrational, unrealistic, problem interfering, solution interfering, task or goal interfering by various authors. Many people hold both helpful and unhelpful underlying beliefs and operate according to the more helpful ones most of the time until precipitating factors trigger the unhelpful beliefs into action. This triggering of unhelpful underlying beliefs by precipitating factors was discussed in the cognitive conceptualization of Chapter 3 where Tom's difficulties were outlined. For people (usually

those with axis I problems such as depression) who already have
helpful beliefs in place, these need to be accessed and built upon.
Specific helpful beliefs are also best named or labelled in the client's
own language. People without significant alternative helpful beliefs
already in place (commonly axis II diagnoses) will almost certainly
require considerably more time for their development. Helpful beliefs
are formulated following the identification of unhelpful beliefs but
before any attempt is made to modify them.

Fifth, the process of helping the client to rate how strongly they
held an automatic thought on a scale of 0–100 was illustrated in
Chapter 4. The re-rating of the thought after socratic questioning
showed a weakening of the original automatic thought. The process
of weakening both automatic thoughts and underlying beliefs is
aided considerably by encouraging the client continually to rate and
re-rate the strength of their unhelpful thoughts and beliefs. Rating
also aids the strengthening of more helpful thoughts and beliefs.
Hence, rating thoughts and beliefs is not only a monitoring tool but a
mechanism for change.

Modifying underlying beliefs

Common interventions

Once one or more significant underlying unhelpful beliefs have been
established and the therapist is confident that the client is now ready
to begin work on them, alternative, more helpful beliefs begin to be
developed. Several factors will indicate to the brief therapist that the
client is ready and that such work is necessary. As noted previously,
work on underlying beliefs may not always be required. First, the
client will have developed a reasonable ability to identify and
question his own automatic negative thoughts and to generate more
helpful alternatives to them. In brief therapy, the client's ability to do
this early in therapy is a prerequisite (see Chapter 3). Second, the
client may be well able to do this work but nevertheless fails to
improve or seems 'stuck'. Each negative automatic thought seems
to be replaced by another, suggesting that the underlying belief is
powerfully active. Third, the client identifies a number of underlying
beliefs as automatic thoughts (see A1, p. 71) and the therapist
considers that the client is ready to work at this deeper level.

Once ready, the therapist encourages the client to generate an
unhelpful underlying belief (by using one or more of the methods
given in items 1 to 8 in section A), provides a rationale for working
with such beliefs (see psychoeducation about underlying beliefs in
section A) and then proceeds to generate an alternative, more helpful

underlying belief. It is preferable for the therapist to generate some possibilities in his own mind and use these to guide the client to identify the most helpful alternatives through the use of socratic dialogue. This form of questioning has been discussed and exemplified in Chapter 4. The aim is to find a more helpful alternative belief which is realistic and believable to the client: if the client and therapist collaboratively agree the alternative belief it is more probable these qualities will be present.

Therapists' views differ concerning the construction of helpful alternative beliefs. Beck (1995: 175) suggests 'a relatively positive belief is generally easier for a patient to adopt than a belief that is at an extreme', whereas Padesky (1994: 270) holds the view that 'since schemas are absolute, the alternative used in therapy should be stated as an absolute statement'. If we take Tom's underlying belief 'I'm unlovable', corresponding alternative beliefs might be 'I'm generally lovable' (a relatively positive belief) and 'I'm lovable' (an absolute statement) respectively. The precise statement collaboratively agreed with the client will ultimately depend on a range of factors which may include the client's personality, personal style and life experience. The pragmatic utility of the belief statement and the extent to which the client is able to believe it will be determining elements.

> *Therapist*: Tom, we've identified the underlying belief 'I'm unlovable' which you seem to believe in quite strongly.
> *Tom*: Yeah.
> *Therapist*: Can you think of an alternative underlying belief which might be more helpful?
> *Tom*: I'm lovable, I suppose.
> *Therapist*: You don't sound too sure about that Tom.
> *Tom*: I'm not sure I could actually really believe that.
> *Therapist*: Is there an alternative belief you could believe?
> *Tom*: Well I think I could believe that I'm lovable to some people some of the time.
> *Therapist*: That sounds more realistic to you then, does it, Tom?
> *Tom*: Yeah. It reminds me of 'you can please some of the people some of the time but you can't please all of the people all of the time'.

Once an alternative helpful belief has been generated, the client and therapist work to modify the unhelpful underlying belief. This involves a process of engaging the client in viewing the world through the framework of the new alternative and helpful belief rather than the old unhelpful belief. To optimize this happening outside therapy, the client is encouraged to enter both the old and the new belief alongside each other in his therapy notebook (discussed in Chapter 4). Being aware of the helpful belief and actually believing in it are quite different. Noting the new belief down in the therapy notebook is a good starting point for the client, but insufficient to bring about change in itself. For this to happen, one or more of a number of techniques are usually called for which are now outlined.

1   Socratic dialogue

The use of questioning as a major therapeutic device (Beck et al., 1979: 66–71) has become the hallmark of cognitive behaviour therapy and is referred to elsewhere in this book as socratic dialogue. It will therefore not surprise you to find that leading the client to a modified belief through the use of such questioning is the first technique on our list. Although this may be useful in modifying beliefs as an intervention of its own, the use of such questioning is also integrated into the other techniques for modifying beliefs and is employed as a general tool throughout therapy. When modifying a particular unhelpful belief the therapist guides the client to examine the operation of the belief in specific situations rather than dealing with the generalized belief in a woolly and global fashion. Through this means, the therapist can lead the client to marshall evidence which refutes the belief in specific situations. This can then be extended to a wider range of situations and generalized as a helpful underlying belief.

One means of moving from the more generalized to the more specific, using socratic questioning, is to help the client to transform his attitudes and rules into conditional assumptions (Beck, 1995). For example, the attitude, 'it's terrible to be unlovable' and the rule, 'I should be lovable' are difficult to modify in this form because they are so general and relate to nothing in particular. The conditional assumption 'If I am unlovable, then I am worthless' is much easier to modify because specific examples in which he considers himself worthwhile can probably be found which lead to the belief 'I am unlovable' being weakened.

> Tom: Yes, I believe strongly 'I should be lovable' [rule] and it's terrible to be unlovable [attitude].
> Therapist: What does it mean to you to be unlovable?
> Tom: Well, it means I am worthless.
> Therapist: So you believe 'if I am unlovable I am worthless' [conditional assumption]. How strongly would you say you believed that statement at this moment?

2   Scaling beliefs

Core beliefs are 'overgeneralized, inflexible, imperative and resistant to change' (Beck et al., 1990b: 29) and intermediate beliefs have similar qualities but to a lesser degree. The use of scales for measuring the extent to which a client holds an unhelpful automatic thought or underlying belief was introduced in Chapter 4 and earlier in this chapter. Such use already challenges rigidity by implying that thoughts or beliefs are not either held or not held; a vast range from no belief to total belief in a thought is possible. Similarly, it is very helpful for a client to recognize that he is, for example, not either lovable or unlovable (all or nothing thinking) but usually somewhere along a range between lovable and unlovable. Where a range exists, change is possible, because it is no longer necessary to occupy one extreme or another.

Scaling beliefs in this way is an important technique for introducing flexibility into the thought patterns of clients, especially those whose thinking is polarized (all or nothing thinking). The unhelpful belief and the helpful belief are first identified. The helpful belief is written at one side of a whiteboard and a line drawn to the other side as shown in Figure 5.3.

$$\text{100\%} \underline{\hspace{6cm} \boldsymbol{x} \underline{\hspace{1cm}} \text{Lovable}}$$
$$\text{100\%} \qquad\qquad\qquad\qquad\qquad\qquad\qquad \text{0\%}$$

Figure 5.3 *Belief scaling*

At one end of the line is placed 0 per cent and at the other 100 per cent as shown. The client is asked to put a cross at the point on the scale they currently occupy. This will initially be towards the extreme of 0 per cent. Through a process of socratic questioning, perhaps coupled with other techniques identified in this chapter, it is usually possible for the client to move towards the more helpful belief. Once the client has accomplished a reasonable shift in belief within the session, the process and the shift are noted in his therapy notebook and home assignments decided upon. This will usually involve the client using the technique with other unhelpful underlying beliefs previously identified. Additionally, behavioural experiments can be used to support and consolidate the newly developed belief (see item 3 which follows).

Belief scaling, also known as the continuum method (Padesky, 1994; Padesky and Greenberger, 1995; Pretzer, 1983) can be used in a variety of ways. For example, a scale ranging from 100 per cent lovable to 100 per cent unlovable is possible but is pragmatically less useful than the scale shown above. Padesky (1994) has used such methods extensively and outlines a number of variations. A useful method she describes is the criteria continuum method which was known by the personal construct theorist, Kelly (1955: 143), as abstracted scales. The client is asked what qualities constitute the positive pole of a scale as shown above. For example, some of the

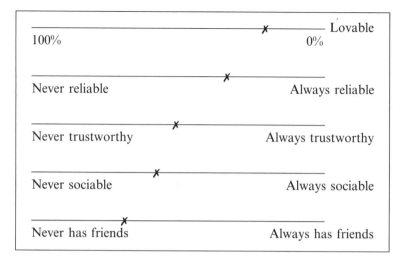

Figure 5.4   *Belief scaling: criteria continuum method*

criteria Tom gave as constituting 'lovableness' were reliable, trust-worthy, sociable and having many friends. A scale showing both extremes for each of these is listed beneath the main 'lovable' scale, and a similar approach is adopted for modifying each of them as is used for the main belief (see Figure 5.4).

It is notable that the scale connects two opposites and in doing so enables a transition from the unhelpful to the helpful belief. In practice the therapist continuously uses scales in her own mind to keep track of the position the client holds for any given belief, irrespective of whether or not the client and therapist are currently using this intervention at any point in therapy. We noted that Kelly used scales in a similar way to that described above and also established fixed role therapy which is described in the next section.

3   Fixed role therapy

A number of therapists outside cognitive behaviour therapy have recognized that if a client can be encouraged to act in a manner which is not in keeping with their unhelpful beliefs, this can lead to a change in the beliefs, which in turn can lead to further changes in behaviour. Such an approach is called fixed role therapy (see Bonarius, 1970; Epting, 1984; Karst and Trexler, 1970; Kelly, 1955; Skene, 1973). This approach is consistent with the cognitive behaviour therapy model which asserts that thoughts, emotions and behaviour are integrated: a change to one will be reflected by changes in the others. The application of this principle is a powerful technique in cognitive behaviour therapy. Once an alternative helpful belief has been identified and agreed with the client, he is led (again through socratic questioning) to identify a number of ways in which he might act if this new and helpful belief were indeed true. Once a number of actions have been identified which are consistent with the new belief, the client is asked to consider if he could carry these out in practice and the therapist also gauges whether or not he considers that the client could act upon these at this point in time. Once collaboratively agreed, these actions are recorded in his therapy notebook and the client adopts the role consistent with his new and helpful beliefs as a between-session assignment. It is important not to make this role too extensive and not endeavour to apply it in situations which are particularly emotionally charged, but to specify it in some detail and limit the work to this role. The client is asked to behave in a way that is consistent with the new belief, even though he may not be fully convinced of the new belief at this stage. Beck calls this technique 'acting "as if"' (Beck, 1995).

Therapist: Tom, you said that 'if I am unlovable then I am worthless'. How much do you believe that now?

Tom: Well I suppose it's getting less but it's still about 60 per cent.

Therapist: How would it be if you believed that even less?

Tom: That would be great, but I'm not sure how I could do it.

Therapist: Well if instead of believing, 'I am unlovable' you believed 'some people find me lovable some of the time', can you picture what you might do differently today, tomorrow or during the week?

Tom: I suppose I could help Kas with the housework or the gardening.

Therapist: Is there anything else?

Tom: I could go with Kas to visit her mother. She would really like that.

Therapist: Would acting in this way change anything?

Tom: It would improve our relationship and I would feel more lovable.

Therapist: So are you saying that if you behaved in a way that was in line with your new belief, 'some people find me lovable some of the time', others would respond more positively to you and in turn you would feel more lovable?

Tom: Yeah, that's right. I can see that.

Therapist: If you can see yourself behaving like this, when do you think you might be able to carry this out?

The therapist and Tom agree on days and times when Tom can try out his new role consistent with the new, more helpful belief and Tom puts these in his therapy notebook. The therapist explains the rationale for fixed role therapy and encourages Tom to behave in a way that is consistent with the new belief even though he may not be fully convinced of it at this stage.

4   Role play

Cognitive therapy happily uses and adapts techniques from other therapeutic disciplines provided their use is consistent with the cognitive model. Some of the role play techniques originated by gestalt therapists (Fagan and Shepherd, 1970; Feder and Ronall, 1980; Perls, 1969a, 1969b, 1973; Polster and Polster, 1973) are useful and powerful in modifying unhelpful beliefs (Beck, 1995; Ellis, 1982; McMullin, 1986; Trower et al., 1988; Young, 1990). They are not usually practised until after the other interventions using socratic dialogue described in this section.

A major use of role play in cognitive behaviour therapy is in the application of countering. McMullin (1986: 3) has noted: 'A single theory underlies all cognitive restructuring techniques that employ countering. This theory states that when a client argues against an irrational thought, and does so repeatedly, the irrational thought becomes progressively weaker.' (You may recall that 'rational' and 'irrational' thoughts are equivalent to thoughts we have described as 'helpful' and 'unhelpful' respectively.) A number of variations exist using countering in role play. The main technique is as follows. The client is helped to make a list of thoughts 'supporting' the unhelpful belief and with the client's collaboration, a parallel list of counter-thoughts is generated. The role play begins with the client adopting the role of the unhelpful thoughts: these are the thoughts which the client is currently using. The therapist argues against each of these in turn, using the counters (or helpful thoughts) generated earlier. As each unhelpful thought is countered, Young (1990) calls this role play technique 'point-counterpoint'. Once the therapist has modelled the countering role in this way, she and the client reverse roles, with the therapist now becoming devil's advocate. Describing this process may sound contrived, but in practice such role play can be easily introduced if approached confidently by the therapist. This technique is variously known as 'devil's advocate disputing' (Dryden, 1995: 158) and 'rational-emotional role-play' (Beck, 1995: 158).

In the technique just described, the client first assumes the role in which he accepts the unhelpful beliefs (with the therapist modelling the 'countering' of each of these in turn) and then takes the role of 'countering' which the therapist has modelled. In the 'empty chair' technique, the client combines these two opposing roles together, by alternately stating the unhelpful belief and then moving over to the empty chair and speaking to it while now adopting the 'countering' role.

5   Behavioural methods

Altering unhelpful beliefs can often be brought about by behavioural change (Emmelkamp et al., 1978) and a number of conditions may be best helped by the major focus of therapy being behaviourally orientated (Roth and Fonagy, 1996). We have noted elsewhere that behavioural experiments can be a powerful challenge to unhelpful automatic thoughts, provided the experiments are carefully designed. A well-known example is to bring about anxiety symptoms through hyperventilation in a therapy session to test out the client's belief that her symptoms are the result of 'heart problems' rather than anxiety symptoms associated with panic (Clark, 1989: 83). In using behavioural experiments, the aim is to elicit some response which contradicts or fails to support a particular thought or belief. In practice, the therapist and client look ahead at the probable consequences to give the best conditions for success to be achieved, paying attention to any practical difficulties or automatic negative thoughts which may prevent the experiment from being carried out. It is important to convey to the client that this is an experiment. Carrying it out is success in itself, irrespective of the outcome. Approaching the experiment in this way is important to ensure the client does not view certain outcomes as failures.

By use of the criteria continuum method described above, we identified that Tom held an underlying belief that he was highly unreliable which supported his core belief that he was unlovable. To further the work done in session, Tom agreed to test out the belief about unreliability between sessions. He would take on the responsibility for the following three tasks in the following week, which he believed would demonstrate considerable reliability if completed. First, he would phone Kas if coming home late. Second, he would carry out his promise of helping with the housework by vacuuming the living room and entrance hall. Third, he would make an appointment with the citizens' advice bureau about debt counselling.

When using behavioural methods, the cognitive model is kept firmly in mind by the therapist. In this way, interventions are set up with a specific purpose which usually includes a practical counter of unhelpful thoughts or beliefs. In some conditions, the experiments may serve other purposes, such as engaging in action where lethargy and lack of motivation are prevalent. Fixed role therapy may be seen as a behavioural method too, since the client is trying out new behaviours consistent with more positive beliefs.

6   Comparing self with others

Comparing self to others can be useful for a number of purposes, two of which are to aid distancing and decentring (Beck, 1967, 1975, 1976; Beck et al., 1979). Distancing is the ability of the client to regard thoughts objectively while decentring is the 'technique of prying the patient loose from his pattern of regarding himself as the focal point of all events' (Beck, 1976: 244).

Like the other techniques described above for modifying beliefs, comparing self with others may be used alone or with other technique(s). Like many other techniques, it is commonly coupled with socratic questioning. Usually, the client is led to think of other people who:

- do not hold the client's unhelpful beliefs but who she regards favourably;

or
- do hold the client's unhelpful beliefs (to their detriment).

These interventions can be powerful tools in helping to shift unhelpful beliefs, by using people well known to the client such as friends, relatives, children and work colleagues. The therapist will help the client to carefully select another who has similar or opposite beliefs depending upon the aim of the particular intervention. For example, a mentor or role model might be chosen. The client can consider the effect of adopting the more helpful beliefs she assumes the mentor to have. She is led to recognize that another does not hold her belief, yet functions more effectively. By comparison, the client recognizes that she can modify her own beliefs without adverse consequences and with probable benefits. An opposite approach is to select another who does hold the unhelpful belief, but suffers as a consequence. It is often easier for the client to generate meaningful, insightful and believable counters to others' unhelpful beliefs than to her own, even when they are the same. This enables distance from the unhelpful belief to be achieved. Once the client has been able to generate and work through more helpful beliefs for another, she is often more able to apply such beliefs to herself.

7   Belief change chart (BCC) and cognitive conceptualization chart (CCC)

The benefits of the client taking an active role in the therapy process have been continually emphasized. This process is aided by the client's use of a therapy notebook. Its use in session can lead to the retention of information out of session and acts as a link to work done by the client in and out of session. The belief change chart (BCC) has a similar purpose and is a means of succinctly recording progress in modifying beliefs (see Appendix 4). It is also a tool for helping the client to monitor her experiences outside sessions and reframing her thinking around them. It is therefore an aid to help the client to become her own therapist. It is usually necessary to begin work on the chart together during the session. These belief change charts enable the client to hold on to and remember new information in a structured way. Several versions of the belief change chart exist, called by different names and including slightly different contents. Examples are the resynthesis worksheet (McMullin, 1986: 154–7); positive data log (Padesky, 1994: 273–7); core belief worksheet (Beck, 1995: 176–82); core belief record (Padesky and Greenberger, 1995: 145–50).

The form is introduced to the client once she and the therapist have together identified a significant unhelpful underlying belief, generated an alternative and gone some way in modifying her unhelpful beliefs using one or more of the interventions outlined above.

The cognitive conceptualization chart (CCC) was introduced in Chapter 3 (Figures 3.3 and 3.5) and is shown as Appendix 3. Its central position in brief cognitive behaviour therapy has been emphasized. We have also noted the usefulness of presenting it to the client early in therapy if appropriate through use of a whiteboard. A CCC may also be a useful tool for the client to demonstrate the development and progression of unhelpful beliefs over time. It can be a powerful and contextualizing artefact, especially for people who tend to think that their present difficulties are caused by their past. Coupled with the belief change chart (BCC), the conceptualization can link the past with the present: old unhelpful beliefs do not have to be carried into the future. They have been learned and seemed plausible at the time but this does not make them accurate. It is now possible to learn new beliefs which are helpful and functional. The CCC indicates that predisposing factors in early development may lead to underlying (unhelpful) beliefs which are later precipitated through a critical incident. Theorists such as Piaget (1954) have proposed that people incorporate logical errors into themes and beliefs developed in childhood which they later continue to accept as reality. McMullin (1986) and Young (1990) recommend the usefulness of exploring the development and progression of unhelpful beliefs from childhood with the client.

A useful technique for doing this uses the belief change chart (BCC). The client is asked to recall situations earlier in her life when the underlying belief appeared to be present. A number of different situations can be found from early life (ranging from childhood to early adolescence) for each underlying belief and these are each recorded on the BCC. The client is then encouraged to find evidence for the new belief for each of these time periods and this is recorded on the chart alongside the evidence for the old belief. Each old belief is then countered, using the third column. Finally, the client is helped to produce a general statement in the space at the bottom of the form combining all this material in a succinct form (see Figure 5.5).

Old belief (unhelpful): *I'm unloveable*

. . . . *65* rate 0–100%

New belief (helpful): *I'm loveable some of the time by some people*

. . . . *40* rate 0–100%

Evidence for new belief rate 0–100%	Evidence for old belief rate 0–100%	Counter to old belief rate 0–100%
Kas wants commitment from me, and must have loveable feelings for me 65%	*Mother abandoned me* 85%	*There were many reasons she was away. It wasn't all down to me. Even if she didn't love me doesn't prove I am unloveable.* 70%
	Father didn't show any love towards me. 65%	*He didn't show any love to anyone!! He was always busy working, but this doesn't mean he didn't love me.* 75%
I've got two close friends who confide in me. 60%		
Nextdoor neighbour frequently calls in to see me. 50%	*Several failed relationships.* 55%	*Although those relationships ended, I think my partners loved me at times. I've come to see there are things about me I need to change, but this doesn't make me unloveable.* 70%
	Constant arguments with Kas. 50%	*I can see my arguments with Kas are like the other relationships. Some things I say and do might not be acceptable, but this doesn't make me unloveable.* 70%
(Specific)	(Specific)	(Specific)

General helpful summary:

I came to see myself as unloveable early on in my life and assumed I was unloveable because those close to me didn't show me any love. But I now realize this says more about them than me. I recognize there are aspects of me I need to work on and this is helping me to accept myself.

Figure 5.5   *Belief change chart (BCC)*

2   The cognitive model process

(b)   Educate client about self-acceptance (as necessary)

A lack of self-acceptance features in a number of unhelpful under-lying beliefs. Although this may be approached through the more general belief modification techniques outlined earlier, it is some-times useful to intervene directly using the types of interventions exemplified below. The central concept to convey to the client is that it is not logical, realistic or helpful to apply global ratings to human beings as we are far too complex. Global ratings are usually but by no means always derogatory, such as 'I am worthless', 'he's an idiot', or 'she's a hopeless parent'. Global ratings are consistent with the thinking error of labelling described under the whistlestop tour of Chapter 2. This form of thinking is also usually consistent with stigmatization (see Goffman, 1963) which applies a global rating to a particular group of people (e.g. ethnic minorities, people with mental health problems or physical disabilities) or a member of such a group. Korzybski (1933), who originated the philosophy of general semantics, suggested that the imprecise use of language often leads to distorted thinking. Traits, aspects and behaviour may be rated, (Dryden, 1991: 276), but not a person's self. It is more helpful for clients to accept themselves and others as fallible human beings.

A helpful technique to convey this principle is the 'Big I, little i' (Ellis et al., 1998: 112–14) based on the concept of the egoless self devised by Lazarus (1977). The therapist first draws a 'Big I' on a whiteboard or sheet of paper (see Figure 5.6).

> *Therapist*: Tom, this 'Big I' represents you. Your totality. In a minute I'm going to fill it up with 'little i's' which stand for various things about you, such as the way you dress, the way you talk, the papers you read, the food you like and so on.
>
> *Tom*: Yeah.
>
> *Therapist*: Now, Tom. Let's start to fill in this 'Big I' with a few things about you. What would Kas, your friends or family say were some of your good points?
>
> *Tom*: Well, I'm kindhearted, er . . . generous, . . . I now help out with the housework and do the gardening! And I've got a good sense of humour.

As Tom identifies various good points about himself, the therapist draws small 'i's' inside the 'Big I' to represent each of them.

> *Therapist*: Each of these 'little i's' stands for some aspect of you. This one (pointing to a 'little i') stands for you being kindhearted, this one down here stands for you being generous and these other 'little i's' stand for the other good points you mentioned you had.

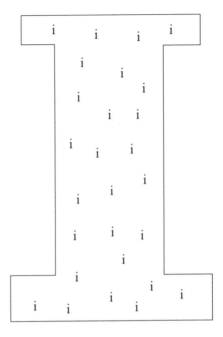

Figure 5.6   *Big I, little i*

The therapist continues to elicit further 'i's' such as the negative things people might say about Tom, the neutral aspects he thinks they may notice as well as qualities and characteristics which Tom identifies about himself, until there are many 'little i's'.

> *Therapist:* Let's return to your problem Tom. You say that you think you are a 'total failure' after your row with Kas and think you could have handled the situation differently. [*Therapist now circles one 'little i' to denote this.*] You say 'because I didn't handle the situation better and have had yet another row with Kas, that proves I'm inadequate'. Think back to what we have been discussing in the last five minutes. Are you actually being accurate?
>
> *Tom:* Well, it was a big row and one of many.
>
> *Therapist:* Okay, it was a big row [*pointing to the 'little i' he had circled in the 'Big I'*] But how does that – this 'little i' – make you [*drawing a circle around the whole 'Big I'*] a total failure, and an inadequate person?
>
> *Tom:* I don't suppose it does really.
>
> *Therapist:* Tom, you may have some difficulties when it comes to communicating with Kas [*pointing to 'little i'*], and you may sometimes act in a way that makes the situation worse [*pointing to another 'little i'*], but as we can see from the diagram [*circles 'Big I'*] this doesn't make you a total failure. We would need all the facts about your whole life from beginning to end to decide if you were a total failure.

Tom: Yeah, well I'm not on my deathbed yet!

Therapist: You're absolutely right. If you were on your deathbed we could open up the big book [*therapist opens up his hands as if opening up a large book*] and count up the number of times you have been a failure in your entire life. 'I was a failure on 9th of June in 1979, I let in a goal during a football match in 1981, I lost my wallet in 1983, I said the wrong thing to Kas and caused a row, I lost my job twice!

Tom: [*laughing*] I think that's enough.

Therapist: Do you think you could summarize what point you think I'm attempting to make?

Tom: I can judge the things I do such as rowing with Kas or acting in a certain way, but I'm too complex a person to be judged as totally inadequate or a complete and utter failure!

Therapist: You're right. You can rate your traits, deeds, appearance, actions, skills or skills deficits but you are too complex to rate your entire self. We may only have all the facts when you are on your deathbed and that may be the time you could rate yourself globally. But even then if we discover you have failed at some or even many things in your life it would still be an impossible task to rate yourself as 'totally inadequate or a complete and utter failure'.

The therapist will need to adapt the model depending upon what particular problem the client brings to therapy. It is important to avoid taking a didactic approach with this technique. By asking socratic questions (see above and Chapter 4) clients usually become actively involved in the method and then provide ample evidence to counter their global negative beliefs about themselves. Ellis et al. (1998) recommended the use of humorous over-exaggeration to help some clients see how absurd it is globally to rate themselves or others.

Visual techniques and interventions are often easier for the client to recall than dialogue when they are distressed about a particular event. Often clients recount how they saw in their mind's eye a picture of the 'Big I–little i' diagram when attempting to counter unhelpful thoughts such as 'I've lost my job therefore I'm a total failure' or 'if I act weak in front of others then that makes me totally weak'. Although the 'Big I–little i' technique is regularly used by therapists, the concept may be better demonstrated using objects in the counselling room or introduced to the session (see Figure 5.7 adapted Palmer, 1997a).

Between-session tasks are negotiated collaboratively with clients as discussed previously to help them strive towards unconditional self-acceptance, for example: bibliotherapy consisting of reading self-help literature on increasing self-acceptance (e.g. Dryden and Gordon, 1990, 1992; Ellis, 1977a, 1988; Ellis and Harper, 1997; Lazarus et al., 1993; Palmer and Burton, 1996); listening to audio cassettes (e.g. Ellis 1977b); use of imagery (Ellis 1979; Maultsby and Ellis 1974);

- Big I little i
- Bowl of fruit (do you throw it all away if one piece has mould?)
- Box of tissues (if one tissue is ripped, are they all?)
- Packet of cigarettes (if one is crushed, are the rest impaired?)
- Box of cigars (ditto)
- Description of room (can whole room be rated by one aspect?)
- Jug of water (can a drop from a jug show the shape or amount within it?)
- Missing hand (is hand whole self?)
- Vase of flowers (if one is wilted, do you discard them all?)
- Shrubs or roses in a garden bed (does one plant describe them all?)
- Car with a flat tyre (do you scrap the car?)
- Post-it stickers (or other sticky paper – different aspects of person written on paper and stuck safely onto the client's clothing)
- Work colleague/friend (acceptance of others' failings but not one's own)
- Draw 3 circles:
  - 'perfect' person (with ticks inside)
  - 'bad' person (with crosses inside)
  - 'fallible' person, i.e. reality (with ticks, crosses and circles, representing neutral aspects, inside)
- Concertina (fold paper with aspects of person written on each section)
- Wardrobe (throw out all clothes if one item disliked?)

Figure 5.7   *Aids to demonstrate self-acceptance (adapted from Palmer, 1997a: 19)*

tape recorded disputing (Ellis et al., 1998); reading coping statements (Cautela, 1971; Goldfried, 1971; Lazarus et al., 1980; Mahoney and Thoresen, 1974; Meichenbaum, 1975, 1977; Suinn and Richardson, 1971) and rational proselytizing (Bard, 1973) in which clients teach principles of helpful thinking to their friends and relatives to consolidate their view of self-acceptance.

Another technique which helps clients towards unconditional self-acceptance is listening to tape recordings of the counselling sessions (Palmer and Dryden, 1995). (Audio recordings of the therapy session have previously been discussed in Chapter 2.) This has a number of benefits for clients such as reinforcement of concepts covered during the therapy session, replaying sections which were not completely understood, reassurance at hearing the therapist countering unhelpful underlying beliefs. The client realizes that the therapist can accept her even if the client is unable to accept herself (role modelling).

3   Help the client to work on problem(s) in and out of therapy

(a)   Pass responsibility for therapeutic work over to client
We have discussed the gradual handing over of responsibility for therapeutic work to the client previously in items 3 and 8 of Chapter 2 and item 8 of Chapter 4. The therapist encourages the client to participate fully and to take over many aspects of therapy from an early stage. This is not to say that the therapist becomes less actively involved, but uses the socratic dialogue and questioning style which leads the client to discover for himself ways of dealing with his difficulties such as identifying the distortions present in his own thinking. It is important for the client to come to the conclusion that he has the ability to examine and question his unhelpful thoughts and beliefs. During this middle stage of therapy the therapist encourages the client to take a more active role within the therapy session by encouraging him to continue to write salient points and assignments in his therapy notebook. We aim to encourage him to choose topics to discuss, summarize the main points discussed and devise between-session tasks during the session. In addition, the client's completion of various sheets and charts (as discussed previously in this chapter and elsewhere) helps to place responsibility for change with the client while developing and consolidating the change process. What is also helpful when passing responsibility over to the client is regularly to review 'where we are in therapy' by asking the client what he has learned so far and what aspects has he found most helpful.

(b)   Encourage client to become own therapist
Encouraging the client to become his own therapist begins during the early stages of therapy and continues throughout (see item 8 of Chapter 2). It develops naturally alongside the client's acceptance of responsibility for therapeutic change. The client is continually encouraged to record in his therapy notebook what he has learned and any new ideas or actions which he has found particularly helpful. (The therapist can also learn from these what the client has not found helpful and this will guide the therapist either to invest more time in conveying and developing a particular concept or to move to something else at this particular time.) These new understandings will benefit and encourage the client to carry out further techniques or tasks outside the therapy session, during and following the completion of therapy. While specific tasks and techniques are negotiated for homework assignments, there is an overarching theme of encouraging the client to *take action* when difficulties occur or emotional

	Steps	Questions or actions
1	Problem identification	What is the concern?
2	Goal selection	What do I want?
3	Generation of alternatives	What can I do?
4	Consideration of consequences	What might happen?
5	Decision-making	What is my decision?
6	Implementation	Now do it!
7	Evaluation	Did it work?

Figure 5.8   *Seven steps and seven questions (Wasik, 1984)*

distress arises, rather than engaging in previously adopted cycles of unhelpful thinking. This taking action encompasses the work we have described elsewhere and may be cognitive or behavioural.

A distinction was drawn previously in Chapter 4 (item 5, p. 52) between emotional problems and practical problems (Bard, 1980) but their interrelationship was also emphasized. Some clients have poor problem-solving skills and may benefit from brief problem-solving training. Several therapists have developed problem-solving approaches within counselling (Hawton and Kirk, 1989; Meichenbaum, 1985; Milner and Palmer, 1998; Palmer, 1994; Spivack et al., 1976) which have similar frameworks for identifying and solving problems. A succinct approach proposed by Wasik (1984) consists of seven steps accompanied by corresponding questions (Figure 5.8).

It is helpful for the client to record their problem-solving processes on paper. A blank form to aid this process is shown in Appendix 5 and a completed worksheet is shown in Figure 5.9.

*(c)   Encourage client to continue with tasks between
        sessions*

Between-session tasks have previously been discussed in *homework setting* (Chapter 2, p. 22) and in *change* (Chapter 4, p. 52). In brief cognitive behaviour therapy great emphasis is placed upon between-session tasks as they help equip the client to deal with difficult situations alone (to become own therapist). It is worth the therapist remembering at this point that between-session tasks remains an important feature throughout therapy and clients who do between-session tasks regularly show greater improvement than those who do not (Niemeyer and Feixas, 1990; Persons et al., 1988). Beck et al. (1979) describe between-session tasks as an 'integral, not optional part of cognitive therapy'. Within each session, the individual tasks which will form the between-session work for the client are collaboratively agreed. This work is reviewed at the next session and may

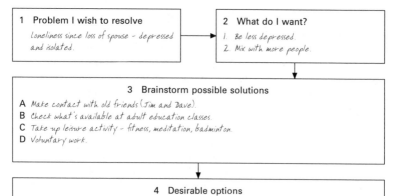

1 Problem I wish to resolve

Loneliness since loss of spouse - depressed and isolated.

2 What do I want?

1. Be less depressed.
2. Mix with more people.

3 Brainstorm possible solutions

A Make contact with old friends (Jim and Dave).
B Check what's available at adult education classes.
C Take up leisure activity - fitness, meditation, badminton.
D Voluntary work.

4 Desirable options

PROS	CONS
A (i) Enjoy their company.	(i) I'm not a part of their lives anymore.
(ii) We have things in common.	(ii) Dave now lives a long way away.
(iii) Making the effort would cheer me up.	(iii) Not much chance to meet others.
(iv)	(iv)
B (i) Might be very enjoyable.	(i) Another bill to pay!
(ii) Opportunity to meet new people.	(ii) I won't know anyone there.
(iii) Gets me out of the house.	(iii) It's a big step for me.
(iv) Isn't too far away.	(iv)
C (i) As in B.	(i) I might be too unfit already.
(ii) Will improve health.	(ii) As in B.
(iii) Keep me occupied.	(iii)
(iv)	(iv)
D (i) Like helping others.	(i) Where do I start; whom do I contact.
(ii) Most of B.	(ii) What could I do?
(iii) Take focus off me.	(iii) Am I up to it?
	(iv)

5 Decide on best solution(s)

Would like to get back in touch with Jim and Dave but want to make new friends too. This might be easiest to do at evening class (wine making?) and/or leisure centre.
Perhaps do voluntary work at a later date.

6 What action will I take?

Phone Jim and Dave on Saturday.
Get adult education brochure at library and ask there about voluntary work.
Go to leisure centre.

7 What happened?

Am meeting Jim next week but Dave is never in.
Got adult education brochure and found that they did badminton too.
Library gave me details of local centre for voluntary service but don't feel ready to contact them yet.

Figure 5.9   *Problem-solving worksheet*

be relatively brief, or take up much of a session if it incorporates issues which the client wishes to discuss. If the between-session tasks are not reviewed regularly then they will probably not be viewed as important by the client and compliance and completion will probably drop off substantially. As therapy progresses assignments may change in emphasis from behavioural to more cognitive work or cognitive work to more behavioural depending on the nature of the client's problems.

Prior to agreeing an assignment, the therapist checks out with the client whether there are any potential obstacles such as negative automatic thoughts associated with its completion. Even so, there will inevitably be occasions when a client experiences difficulties with an assignment and this will need to be discussed and explored with the client within the session. This discussion may lead the therapist to discover that the assignment had been too difficult or not clearly defined in the first place, or was hindered by the client's negative thinking. With frank and open discussion the therapist will have an opportunity to assess the appropriateness of the assignment and convey to the client that she is concerned with devising specific assignments which are tailormade for him. If the therapist had been too optimistic regarding what she thought the client could achieve, this will provide an opportunity for the therapist to admit that she made a mistake. This will further build upon the therapeutic alliance and enhance rapport.

(d) Prepare client for setbacks and ending therapy – lapse and relapse reduction

Preparation for dealing with future difficulties begins in the first session and continues in subsequent sessions, alongside preparation for ending therapy. In this middle stage of therapy more emphasis is put upon dealing with setbacks and relapse reduction. Some explanation is beneficial regarding the 'ups and downs' of the therapy process. For example, it will be beneficial to explain to a client that his progress probably will fluctuate throughout therapy and lapses will inevitably occur, this being a normal path for recovery. By explaining this it is hoped that the client will be more prepared for setbacks and be less likely to catastrophize if they occur. Setbacks during therapy provide an opportunity for the client to practice skills which have been learnt in therapy. The process of overcoming lapses or relapses during therapy helps equip him to handle them when and if they occur after therapy. In some cases the client is able to identify situations in the future which may lead to difficulties or potential setbacks. In these circumstances the client and therapist can work together to devise an action plan of how to cope with such situations.

It is helpful to reflect on specific techniques which the client has found helpful and been successful in implementing so far in therapy.

In other cogitive therapy literature often the term relapse prevention occurs. We prefer the term reduction as this is more realistic and does not set the client up to fail as brief lapses or relapses are possible.

Practice points

1 Use the cognitive conceptualization and therapist's goals to guide the course of therapy.
2 Use the goals as a checklist between sessions to plan future work.
3 Continue to maintain collaborative therapeutic relationship.
4 Continue to give positive feedback and encouragement.
5 Shift focus of therapy from negative automatic thoughts to intermediate and core beliefs (as necessary).
6 Use the methods and materials presented in this chapter to identify and modify underlying beliefs (as necessary).
7 Educate client about self-acceptance (as necessary).
8 Pass responsibility for therapeutic work over to client.
9 Encourage client to become own therapist using material recorded in his therapy notebook. Help client to distinguish between psychological and practical problems and apply problem-solving techniques to the latter.
10 Encourage client to continue with tasks between sessions.
11 Prepare client for setbacks and ending therapy – lapse or relapse reduction (prevention).

6
End Stage of Therapy

The structure of therapy was introduced and developed in Chapters 4 and 5 under three main themes:

1 Collaborative therapeutic relationship.
2 Cognitive model process.
3 Help client to work on problem(s) in and out of session.

We will continue to use this framework in the present chapter to introduce and explain the goals of therapy in its final stages. We also emphasized that these themes overlap, as do the goals which form their content; nor are the beginning, middle and end stages isolated from each other. Brief cognitive behaviour therapy is a developmental process in which the focus of therapy changes over time while the cognitive conceptualization and fundamental characteristics give it consistency. This process of therapy is depicted in Figure 6.1.

In the beginning and middle stages of therapy, clients will have already worked outside the therapy session and the therapist will have been mindful not to have moved on to new material until an existing piece of work has been adequately mastered. At the end stage of therapy the focus moves to consolidating past gains and encouraging the client to work independently. These two aspects of consolidation and client independence generate the therapist's goals forming the content of the themes previously stated at the start of

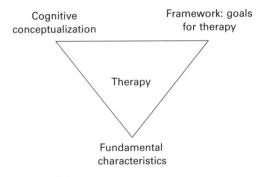

Figure 6.1   *Process of therapy*

1 *Collaborative therapeutic relationship*
(a) Prepare client for ending of therapy.
(b) Consider dependency issues.

2 *The cognitive model process*
(a) Client summarizes what has been learnt and understands
     appropriate techniques and tools.
(b) Therapist attributes value to client's efforts.
(c) Decide when to end therapy consistent with development of
     cognitive conceptualization.
(d) Explore obstacles to ending.

3 *Help the client to work on problem(s) in and out of therapy*
(a) Client to be own therapist.
(b) Lapse and relapse reduction: develop action plan for potential
     problems.

Figure 6.2   *Therapist's goals: end stage of therapy*

this chapter and presented in Figure 6.2. We will now consider each
of the goals from this figure.

1   Collaborative therapeutic relationship

(a)   Prepare client for ending of therapy
Preparing the client to end therapy starts early in the brief cognitive
behaviour therapy process. You may find it helpful to remind
yourself of the fundamental characteristics of cognitive behaviour
therapy outlined in Chapter 2. The client is encouraged to take an
active role in therapy within each session and by working on tasks
between sessions. This facilitates the planning of therapy and the
planning of its end. The client and therapist work together on each
step of the therapy process. The therapist gives an early indication of
the estimated length of therapy to prepare the client for its end and
reminds the client of the remaining length of therapy at various
points throughout the process. Brief cognitive behaviour therapy
does not, by definition, continue indefinitely and does not work with
every problem the client may have, but focuses on important client
goals (see Chapter 4, p. 59). By working effectively on a few problems, the client will learn new skills which can be applied to other
problematic situations. For some clients, work at the automatic
thought level will lead to sufficient change for therapy to end. Others
will require work at the level of underlying beliefs as discussed in

Chapter 5 and the new beliefs will lead to change in other parts of the client's life. Summaries and feedback (see Chapters 4 and 5) by both therapist and client are also useful in identifying what has been achieved and which goals need further work. As ever, the client records salient points in his therapy notebook.

(b)   Consider dependency issues
Trower et al. (1988) suggest that clients may have two main concerns about the ending of therapy. First, they will be unable to make cognitive behaviour therapy work for them on their own. Second, they need the therapist's emotional support. If such beliefs are apparent, they can be examined and questioned in the same way as other unhelpful beliefs in the manner discussed previously in earlier chapters.

> *Therapist*: Do you have any concerns about ending our sessions together?
> *Tom*: Yes. I feel quite anxious about it. I'm not sure I can cope.
> *Therapist*: What thoughts are going through your mind when we talk about the ending of therapy?
> *Tom*: I just don't feel I can cope without your help, I couldn't cope with becoming unwell again.
> *Therapist*: That sounds like an unhelpful belief and an unhelpful prediction. Let's see if there is any evidence for that and evaluate it.
> *Tom*: Perhaps I'm catastrophizing, but things have been going well with the therapy despite its ups and downs and I feel like I'm getting somewhere. I couldn't stand it if I got unwell again.
> *Therapist*: Let's look at how you have coped in therapy when difficulties have arisen. [*Therapist and client review some examples where unhelpful automatic thoughts have occurred and Tom has responded to them generating more helpful alternatives, using the dysfunctional thought form, which enabled him to see that he has been able to help himself to feel better.*]
> *Tom*: I suppose I do know how to handle my problems and I realize that I might experience some difficult times, but if I write things down on the forms and re-read my therapy notes, it does really help me and I probably could cope even when things get tough.

2   The cognitive model process

(a)   Client summarizes what has been learnt and
understands appropriate techniques and tools
By the end stage of therapy the client will ideally have mastered the cognitive model sufficiently to be able to understand his own problems within its framework and to apply some of the techniques and tools to these problems. The range of techniques and tools that the client might require and be able to apply will vary considerably depending on factors such as the type and extent of the client's

problems, how long he has had them, the depth to which it has been necessary to work (i.e. at the automatic thought level, the intermediate belief level or the core belief level), personality factors, his degree of general understanding, intelligence, insight, and so on. It is highly unlikely that it would be necessary for any client to be familiar with or find it helpful to use all the techniques we have described. It is preferable for him to be confident in the use of a few which he has already applied to his problems and found particularly helpful. Of course, some tools which encapsulate the primary principles of the cognitive model (rather than aspects of it) such as thought forms, will be necessary for almost all clients. The approach will need to be creatively adapted with clients who experience difficulty in writing. Often the use of short 'collapsed' coping statements will be an adequate substitute (see Chapter 7).

Summaries have been mentioned at various points in this book such as the therapist's summary of an 'event' the client has revealed in therapy, using some of the client's own words or phrases where these are significant. Summaries are an important means of consolidating material and strengthening ideas or concepts. We have also seen in previous chapters that the client is encouraged to use summaries too. For example, where the therapist introduces a new therapeutic concept, he is asked in session to summarize what the therapist has said to ensure that she has conveyed her meaning clearly. He is also routinely asked to enter such summaries in his 'therapy notebook' and to summarize the content of a particular session at its close. In addition, a number of the tools and techniques require the client to summarize what has been learnt. For example, the automatic thought form is a tool which implicitly leads the client to summarize an emotional episode, as does the technique of comparing self to others introduced in Chapter 5. Later in this chapter we outline a technique in which the client implicitly summarizes in imagery the essential elements pertaining to his problem (p. 104).

Once the therapist is reasonably confident that the client has sufficient working knowledge of the cognitive model process to be able to apply it to his problems without prompting from the therapist, she will plan a session in which the client considers a number of potential difficulties consistent with his therapeutic goals and works through them in session.

(b)   Therapist attributes value to client's efforts
We have seen that cognitive behaviour therapy has a significant behavioural element and uses behavioural techniques consistent with the cognitive therapy model (Beck et al., 1979: 117–41). As

noted previously, the therapist consistently uses positive reinforcement (Skinner, 1953) in cognitive behaviour therapy by praising the client for any gains made, no matter how small. These gains include changes in the client's understanding of his problems in cognitive terms. By praise, we do not mean an excessive, over-the-top response from the therapist, which may be regarded as patronising and insincere, but a true acknowledgement of the client's progress. At the end stage of therapy these acknowledgements are combined and the therapist summarizes for the client the gains she believes he has accomplished and gives recognition for the effort this has involved. The therapist's summary will follow the client's to avoid pre-empting any material he may wish to bring to the session.

> *Tom*: At last I feel that my life is changing for the better. I have had a much happier and calmer week.
> *Therapist*: I'm pleased to hear that Tom. What do you think has contributed to you feeling 'happier and calmer' this week?
> *Tom*: Well, I kept a record of my unhelpful thoughts and successfully managed to challenge them when they occurred. I have also been much more active as a means of distracting myself when I felt things starting to build up between Kas and me. I either went for a walk or got on with some of the house chores.
> *Therapist*: Do you think the way you are feeling this week is down to you choosing to act differently by changing your behaviour and working on your unhelpful thoughts?
> *Tom*: Yes. I think so.
> *Therapist*: What does this show you about the progress you've made?
> *Tom*: Well, before, I didn't think before I acted and it led me into lots of problems and I let my thoughts run away with me. Now, I am changing that and starting to feel better.

(c)   Decide when to end therapy consistent with
development of cognitive conceptualization

At the beginning of this chapter (p. 98), we stressed that the client is made aware from the start of therapy of its short-term nature and its focus on particular goals and is also reminded during the course of therapy of when it will probably end. This conveys to the client that therapy is a planned process. Introducing the cognitive model to the client further supports that therapy is intentional and planned. From this it follows that therapy will end when the model has been sufficiently (not perfectly) mastered and applied to the client's problems and goals collaboratively agreed between client and therapist from the beginning. However, some clients will wish to extend therapy beyond this point and have the therapist apply it to an ever-widening circle of new problems. If this is so, the therapist may have underestimated the extent and depth of the client's problems and accepted him for brief cognitive behaviour therapy inappropriately. Where this is the case, it may be beneficial to accept the client for longer term cognitive behaviour therapy. (This can present difficulties for the client, particularly if he is paying for therapy himself.) Alternatively, it may be that the client has concerns about ending therapy which can be addressed through the cognitive model itself (see p. 100 and section (d) below).

(d)   Explore obstacles to ending
This section is best read in conjunction with 1(b) and 2(c). Where the client appears reluctant to end therapy, shows some emotion such as sadness or anger or is flippant about it ending, this is best explored with him. An obvious way to do this is to raise it with him to discover what automatic thoughts he may be having. Depending on the work which has already been done with the client, his response to ending may be consistent with unhelpful underlying beliefs already addressed in previous sessions. Whether working at the automatic thought level, the intermediate belief level or the core belief level, this work will not differ significantly from that described in earlier chapters of this book.

3   Help the client to work on problem(s) in and out of therapy

(a)   Client to be own therapist
Encouraging the client to internalize the process of working on his own problems is a very important aspect of brief cognitive behaviour therapy which we have addressed at many points in this text. Empowering the client in this way is an aspect of therapy which is not left until the end stage, but started at the earliest possible opportunity. This is important because it enables the client to be supported as he develops his skills as a self-therapist. Where the client's problems are quite limited and the length of therapy very short, there may be little time available for him to develop such skills. In such circumstances, the therapist may recommend self-help (Ruddell and Curwen, 1997) which may take the form of a self-help group or self-help materials such as *Mind Over Mood: A Cognitive Therapy Treatment Manual for Clients* (Greenberger and Padesky, 1995) or *The Feeling Good Handbook* (Burns, 1989). By the end stage of therapy, maximum responsibility is passed over to the client so that when therapy comes to an end he is best prepared to work independently on further difficulties as they arise.

*(b)   Lapse and relapse reduction: develop action plan for
         potential problems*

Lapse and relapse reduction has been discussed in Chapter 5, p. 96. The process started in the middle stage of therapy continues in this final stage and now becomes more crucial. However, it is really in the beginning and middle stages of therapy that the foundations are laid for successful work at this stage to be possible and most effective. During the earlier stages of therapy the client is guided towards taking an active role in the therapeutic process. At this stage, the client is assisted in developing an action plan which he can put into effect if further difficulties ensue after the current series of sessions with the therapist have ended. Depending on the nature and extent of the client's problems, it is often beneficial to arrange some follow-up or booster sessions at approximately three, six and twelve months. The rationale for these is to check out with the client how her self-therapy work is progressing and to fine-tune any aspect as necessary. Arranging such sessions can be very important for some clients as they make the ending of therapy less final and provide an opportunity for the client to feel that help is at hand if needed. If she believes that the session is no longer necessary nearer the time, she may cancel it.

The action plan for potential problems is started at the end of the penultimate session and developed by the client as a home assignment in preparation for the final session in which it is discussed and developed further if necessary. To aid the development of the action plan, the *preparing for setbacks form* shown fully completed in Figure 6.3 (and as a blank version at Appendix 6) is partially completed by the client in the penultimate session with minimum prompting from the therapist. It is completed by the client prior to the final session as a home assignment. The intention of the 'What I can do' column is to prompt the client to do one or more of the things she has previously done in therapy, as recorded in her therapy notebook and assignment sheets. However, she may also record practical solutions to potential problems. The intention of the action plan is not solely to develop solutions (although these may be very helpful), but to convey and emphasize that future problems, like current difficulties, can be addressed and require the client to be proactive and take action.

In the final session, the preparing for setbacks form is put on the agenda as a major item and discussed fully. After doing so, it is often helpful for the client to rehearse enacting the action plan in imagery: this is a form of coping imagery (Meichenbaum, 1977). To do so, the therapist first talks the client into a state of physical and mental relaxation using a standard procedure (such as the one described in

Use this form to identify possible setbacks before they occur and to work through what you can do in these situations.

Possible setbacks	My unhelpful response	What I can do – helpful response
Within first month Returning to full-time work having been part-time while unwell.	To 'blow-up' when pressurized.	1. Take steps to prevent the work piling up – see supervisor sooner rather than later. 2. Take steps to calm down – use quick relaxation. 3. Check therapy notebook re: our work on perfectionism/Big I little i
Within three months In-laws at Christmas.	Put pressure on myself and don't enjoy it. End up snapping at everyone.	1. What am I telling myself? Examine unhelpful thoughts about perfectionism (use thought form) 2. Be kind to myself - enjoy! 3. Let others help with the work.
Within six months End of year accounts (March). Big pressure at work.	I will tell myself 'I can't cope'.	1. Use the self-help questions to examine unhelpful thinking (Appendix I). 2. Focus on what I <u>can</u> do and not on what I can't do – I've coped well in the past. 3. This will seem insignificant in a couple of months!
Within one year Children on school holidays.	HELP! Too many demands.	1. Use problem-solving worksheet to help plan the time. 2. Let go! Allow others to take some of the responsibility. 3. Remember my helpful new belief about perfectionism and review supporting evidence.

Checklist of some things you can do

Go through therapy notebook – find similar situation and note what you found helpful. Select three most helpful things and apply them to this situation. Use cognitive conceptualization; automatic thought form; problem-solving worksheet; belief change chart; step back from the situation; use relaxation; phone good friend; make fresh appointment; consider how terrible the event will be in six months' time.

Figure 6.3 *Preparing for setbacks*

Chapter 7, p. 137). He then guides her to picture the whole process from the beginning of the problem situation through to taking the appropriate action as outlined in *preparing for setbacks*. It is important for the client to imagine the whole process through to the successful completion of the action plan and for her to picture the details of this process *as she intends it to be*.

Practice points

1   The final stage of therapy focuses on consolidation and client independence.
2   Prepare the client to end therapy and consider dependency issues.
3   Focus on client's understanding of what has been learnt in therapy and attribute value to the client's efforts.
4   Use the cognitive conceptualization to decide when to end therapy and address any obstacles to ending.
5   Develop action plan for potential problems using the skills and knowledge the client has developed as a 'self-therapist'.
6   Consider increasing the length of time between sessions.
7   Build in follow-up or booster sessions.

7
Additional Strategies and Techniques

In the previous chapters we have introduced a number of strategies and techniques that can be used at different stages of therapy. However, we were concerned not to include too many possible interventions in case they blurred the process of therapy which we were keen to depict. In this chapter we include strategies, techniques and interventions that we have found particularly useful and effective when practising brief cognitive behaviour therapy. We do not consider some of the techniques such as relaxation to be 'elegant' as they do not necessarily help the client directly to examine his or her thinking processes. However, when practising brief, time or session-limited therapy a pragmatic approach is recommended and 'inelegant' techniques that help the client to deal with their current problem or difficulties should be considered as a viable option.

The chapter is divided into three technique sections:

- Cognitive/Imaginal
- Behavioural
- Relaxation.

The techniques and interventions should be used as part of the cognitive formulation and not in isolation. The techniques are suitable for a range of problems and disorders. However, some of the techniques such as rational-emotive imagery can trigger high levels of anxiety in some clients. Extreme care should be taken when using these types of techniques if the clients have the conditions listed below:

- asthma attacks triggered by stress/anxiety
- seizures triggered by stress/anxiety
- cardiac condition or other related medical conditions
- depression with suicidal ideation
- hysteria
- pregnant women
- severe psychiatric disorders.

If cognitive behaviour therapy is still indicated, then the application of strategies and techniques that do not trigger high levels of anxiety such as relaxation exercises or coping imagery should be considered more appropriate. In these cases it is recommended that the therapist liaises with the client's medical practitioner with regard to specific interventions.

COGNITIVE/IMAGERY TECHNIQUES

Anti-future shock imagery

This imagery technique was developed by Lazarus (1984) to help clients deal with predicted life events and changes. Common examples are redundancy, death of partner/parents and retirement. Clients are asked to visualize themselves coping with different aspects of the future feared event. For example, Jayne was anxious about how she was going to cope when her employers moved location the following year. She did not want to move to another part of the country, yet if she stayed in London she would effectively become redundant. Before the exercise was attempted, Jayne discussed with the counsellor possible ways of dealing with the problem when the inevitable job loss occurred. This included brainstorming possible coping strategies that she could use. Then the counsellor asked Jayne to visualize coping with the feared event by applying the coping strategies previously discussed. This procedure helped Jayne to reduce how badly she saw the possible outcome and to foresee that nearer the time she would be in a position to find another job. In fact, she came to realize during this process that she could start job hunting immediately although she would lose her redundancy money if she left prematurely. She found this exercise empowering and reported that she 'felt in control of the situation again'.

The technique can be used as a lapse or relapse reduction technique in the ending stage of therapy to help clients cope with future unexpected problems.

Aversive therapy

In this technique an unpleasant image is linked with a stimulus that triggers an undesirable response (Cautela, 1967). This helps the client to reduce or stop the frequency of times he or she undertakes the undesirable response. Milner and Palmer (1998) provide two examples of when this technique has been used: when a client on a stop-smoking programme is offered a cigarette by a friend and she immediately visualizes tar accumulating in the lungs; it may reduce the likelihood of the cigarette being accepted. A client on a weight-control programme can imagine somebody she dislikes vomiting over the food she is about to eat. The therapist negotiates with the client the most suitable image that may help to reduce the undesired behaviour. Whenever possible, it is preferable for the client to choose the unpleasant image. The therapist trains the client in the session to visualize the negative image as vividly as possible. Due to the effect of habituation, if a client visualizes the negative image for a prolonged period, then her abhorrence may subside. Therefore, we recommend that clients are instructed not to use the visualization for longer than five minutes at a time.

Bibliotherapy

In brief cognitive behaviour therapy bibliotherapy is a key intervention. It consists of the client utilizing relevant self-help manuals, books, leaflets, audio-tapes, videos and CDs at the therapist's suggestion (see p. 91). This can help clients to understand the nature of their particular problem and, subsequently, how to deal with it. Self-help material focusing on how cognitive behaviour therapy can be used to treat anxiety and depression is invaluable (e.g. Burns, 1980, 1989) and the literature can be read as a between-session assignment. It is important for the therapist to go through any issues or misunderstandings that may arise from the assignment in the following therapy session. One of the advantages of this intervention is that it can be readily adapted to the client's situation and abilities. Milner and Palmer (1998) have found that clients with reading difficulties can usually use audio-tapes or videos instead of written materials. However, therapists need to maintain a library of self-help books, health-related materials and low cost audio-tapes and videos that clients can either borrow or purchase (see p. 91).

Collapsed coping statements

Once clients have developed helpful coping statements they are usually more prepared to confront their problems. However, long-winded coping statements can be difficult to remember when a client is experiencing pressure and feels anxious. Therefore helpful beliefs need to be shortened or 'collapsed', preferably into one or two words that have personal meaning for the client and are easy to recall.

For example, Sara was anxious about giving feedback to a member of staff in case it was not well received. Her assumption was, 'If I don't have others' approval then I'm hopeless.' The helpful belief she and her therapist developed was, 'Although I like other people's approval, I don't need it. It does not prove that I am hopeless.' Once she felt comfortable with the helpful belief she was asked how she could collapse it, but still, in her mind, retain the message. As this can be a very idiosyncratic process it is recommended that the therapist allows the client to think of a powerful statement herself without too much input or advice. In this example Sara suggested a swear word that she could relate to, 'Sod it!' It is important for the therapist to check out with the client how the collapsed statement will actually help her in the situation. To Sara, in just two words the powerful message conveyed was that she did not need people's approval to survive and if her member of staff was unhappy about the situation then that was his problem and not hers. As a between-session assignment Sara used coping imagery to visualize dealing with seeing him disapprove of her at the meeting and simultaneously imagine saying loudly in her mind, 'Sod it!' She was cautioned about accidentally verbalizing the collapsed statement in the real-life situation.

Coping imagery

This technique allows the client to visualize himself coping with an anticipated difficult situation. It has been used for many different scenarios: for example, being assertive with significant others; driving tests; public speaking; sitting exams. Initially, the therapist discusses with the client what they both believe would be the most suitable behaviour that could be used in a specific situation (Milner and Palmer, 1998). Once agreed, in the session the client closes her eyes and imagines coping with the situation, from the beginning to the end of the event. Coping and *not* mastery is the key word with this technique as many clients will not believe that they could master their problem immediately, if ever, whereas learning how to cope with adversity is considered more realistic. For example, a client who is anxious about giving a presentation to her work colleagues would visualize giving an acceptable, but not perfect, performance. If one of her fears was about being unable to answer difficult questions, she would visualize this occurring but would develop a way of dealing with the situation such as by stating that, 'I'm unsure of the answer to that particular question. However, I'll contact you after the meeting with the answer.'

The client would regularly repeat the exercise as a homework assignment. If the practitioner talks the client through the visualization in the training session it can be tape recorded. The client could listen to the recording for the between-session assignment.

Cost-benefit analysis of beliefs

In behaviour therapy cost-benefit analysis of specific unhelpful behaviours or habits may help a client to assess whether it is worth continuing the stated behaviour. In cognitive behaviour therapy the emphasis is more on the benefits of unhelpful and helpful beliefs. Once the unhelpful belief has been elicited it is written on Form 1 (see Appendix 7). Then the client and therapist note down in the appropriate columns the advantages and disadvantages of the unhelpful belief and develop a more constructive helpful belief. This is written on Form 2 (see Appendix 8). The process is repeated focusing on the advantages and disadvantages of the new helpful belief. This helps the client to consider the benefits of relinquishing the unhelpful belief and accepting a helpful belief. The method can be used with automatic thoughts, thinking errors, intermediate and core beliefs.

Sufficient time should be allocated to completing Form 1. In some cases there are so many disadvantages that the exercise is continued on the reverse side of the handout. Therefore the first part of this exercise could take in excess of thirty minutes. If there is insufficient time left in the session to complete Form 2, then a between-session assignment could be for the client to use Form 1 for other unhelpful beliefs. The following session could focus on completing Form 2. Initially it is important for the therapist to guide the client through both forms to ensure that he or she understands how they are used.

Due to the relatively simple and pragmatic nature of this intervention, it is excellent for brief cognitive behaviour therapy. Once the client has practised using the forms with the assistance of the therapist, then they can be used as self-help tools in between-therapy sessions.

De-catastrophizing continuum

When clients are clearly over-estimating the negative outcome of events, either anticipated or real, often they are making thinking errors such as magnification and all-or-nothing thinking. Instead of just considering the possible outcome as 'difficult, but not the end of the world' they tend to use phrases such as 'it's the end of the world', 'it will be terrible', 'awful', 'horrendous' or 'horrible'. They may use idiosyncratic words or phrases which essentially convey the same meaning such as 'Oh God!' De-catastrophizing is a technique to demonstrate to clients that although bad things may happen, they are seldom (if ever) the end of the world, i.e. worse than bad. By using a continuum of badness scale from 1 to 99.9 the therapist asks the client to state how bad the situation will be. We recommend that the therapist uses either a large sheet of paper or whiteboard for this exercise to plot the relative scores (see Figure 7.1). The latter allows for adjustments to be easily made.

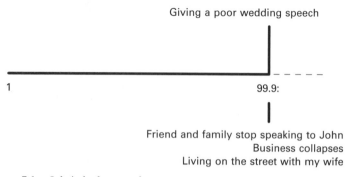

Figure 7.1   *John's badness scale*

A typical transcript of a counselling session illustrates the therapist de-catastrophizing a client's fears about not giving a good 'best man's' speech at a wedding.

John: It will be really terrible if I did not give a good speech at my old college friend's wedding. I feel so anxious about it now that I'm even considering giving him an excuse why I can't go to the wedding.

Therapist: John, if you felt less anxious about giving the speech would you feel better about going.

John: Of course.

Therapist: If I could show you that it would not be 'terrible' if you gave just an average or even below average speech would you feel less anxious.

John: Well, I suppose so although I can't see how you can help me.

Therapist: Would you like to explore this issue a little further?

John: Okay, it's worth a try.

Therapist: When you are feeling really anxious about giving the speech, on a scale of 1 to 99.9, where 99.9 is really bad, how bad is it giving a poor wedding speech?

John: Off the Richter scale. 120! [*Humorously.*]

Therapist: [*laughs*] Obviously, on a scale of 1 to 99.9 you can not go any higher than 99.9.

John: Okay. It feels so bad that it must be at 99.9. [*Therapist draws line on the badness scale to represent giving a poor wedding speech.*]

Therapist: I would like to bring to your attention that logically at that moment in time when you are really anxious you believe that nothing worse could actually happen to you as you have scored 99.9?

John: Hmmm. I suppose so.

Therapist: Just think for the moment. Could anything worse happen?

John: If I gave a poor wedding speech, my friend and his family may never speak to me again.

Therapist: Let's suppose that did happen. On a scale of 1 to 99.9 how bad would that be?

John: Off the end scale again! 150.

Therapist: Ah, but John. I said earlier that . . .

John: I know what you're going to say: You can't go higher than 99.9. Them not speaking to me must also be 99.9. [*Therapist adds this score to the diagram.*]

Therapist: Good. You seem to be getting the hang of this method. Let's assume that they do stop talking to you, what else could happen that would be worse?

John: Well I neglected to tell you that he is my business partner. If we stopped talking, the business would grind to a halt. In fact it could collapse!

Therapist: How bad would that be?

John: 99.9!! [*Therapist adds this score to the diagram.*]

Therapist: If your business collapsed what would be the possible outcome?

John: My wife and I could end up on the streets and that would be really terrible, 200 on the scale!

Therapist: On a scale of 1 to 99.9 it can only be a maximum of 99.9. [*Therapist adds this score to the diagram.*]

John: Hmmm.

Therapist: Have you noticed how everything you are scoring is at the high end of the scale. According to the way you rate things giving a poor wedding speech is as bad as living on the streets with your wife! Have you any thoughts about this?

John: I can see your point. My scale isn't realistic. It needs re-scoring.

Therapist: I agree. Let's have another go at it. If we leave living on the streets with your wife at 99.9, then how would you score your business collapsing?

John: About 85. [*Therapist adds this to new score to the diagram.*]

Therapist: What about your friend and his family not speaking to you?

John: I suppose it can only be about 60.

Therapist: And giving a poor wedding speech?

John: Well, put like this, it can only be about 30.

Therapist: What do think was the point of this exercise? [*Therapist checking that the client has understood this difficult concept.*]

John: When I'm telling myself things such as giving poor wedding speeches would be 'terrible' I make myself anxious and make a huge mountain out of a molehill. Things may be relatively bad, but not really terrible. When I think about all the things that could go wrong in life then this is only passing irritation.

Therapist: I agree. In fact now that you view the situation differently how might your approach to the problem differ?

John: Instead of becoming so anxious about screwing up and avoiding thinking about it, with your help perhaps we could discuss the content of the speech and get down to business.

Therapist: Sounds a good idea to me.

The de-catastrophizing continuum scale (Figure 7.2) allows the client to reassess how bad situations really are and to keep problems in perspective. This can also be beneficial as the client is more likely to focus on dealing with the problem and not waste precious time being anxious or procrastinating. However, we would recommend caution when using it with personally very significant issues such as bereavement or loss of a partner through separation in case the client views

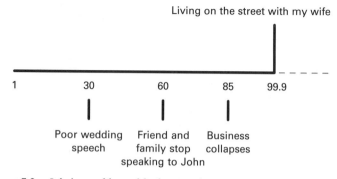

Figure 7.2   *John's recalibrated badness scale*

the therapist as being insensitive which could lead to attrition (i.e. premature termination of counselling).

Deserted Island technique

Understandably not all clients see why it may be beneficial to modify unhelpful beliefs or task interfering cognitions (TICs). Palmer (1993a) has developed the 'Deserted Island' technique to demonstrate to clients that holding on to unhelpful beliefs and not necessarily the activating event can lead to a heightened emotional disturbance and trigger emotions such as anger, guilt, anxiety or depression. This makes the process of assessment easier. Palmer (1993a) described a typical transcript of a therapy session using the Deserted Island technique as below:

> *Therapist:* Now I've shown you the ABC model of cognitive therapy, you still do not seem very convinced that our thoughts, beliefs, rules and attitudes contribute to how we feel about stressful events or situations. If it's okay with you can I spend a few minutes demonstrating to you how this process works?
>
> *Client:* Yeah, fine.
>
> *Therapist:* I find it useful if we move away from a client's problem to illustrate the influence of our thoughts upon how we feel. Let's say, for example, you've been left on a deserted island. You have all your needs such as accommodation and food met, but one thing you don't have on the island are any friends. Imagine being on the island and you hold the belief: I really would prefer to have a friend with me on the island but I don't have to have one. How would you emotionally feel about your situation?
>
> *Client:* I suppose I would be concerned I didn't have anybody to share it with.
>
> *Therapist:* Now, let's say that you're still on the same island but this time your belief is: I must, I must, I really must have a friend on the island. How would you feel this time?

Client: Hmmm. Pretty anxious!

Therapist: Let's just stay with this for a moment. Just imagine that a plane flies over and a friend of yours jumps out and parachutes slowly towards the deserted island. Now imagine that you are still holding the belief: I must, I must, I really must have a friend on the island. How do you feel now?

Client: Very relieved.

Therapist: After a period of time, let's imagine that you are still holding the belief: I must, I must, I really must have a friend on the island. Don't forget, you've still got your friend on the island with you. Can you foresee anything that could happen that you could become upset about again?

Client: I suppose that the friend could be taken away.

Therapist: So even though you have your friend on the island, after a period of time your anxiety might return, especially if you feared that your friend could be taken away.

Client: Yeah.

Therapist: I wonder what your behaviour would be like?

Client: Knowing me I'd be all clingy just in case he was going to leave.

Therapist: Would that help your relationship?

Client: I doubt it. He's more likely to want to leave if he had the chance!

Therapist: Let's change it slightly again. You're still on the same island and your friend is there and this time you're holding the belief: I really would prefer to have a friend with me on the island but I don't have to have one. Would you feel anxious this time?

Client: No. I'd feel much better.

Therapist: Why? [*Therapist checking out whether the client has understood the model.*]

Client: Because I was not insisting that I must have a friend with me.

Therapist: Can you see that in each example I've described similar situations? The only difference has been your beliefs and the different beliefs evoked a different intensity of emotions and possibly different behaviours too. The 'must' belief led to you feeling 'pretty anxious', while the more flexible preference belief led you to feeling just 'concerned'.

Client: Yeah.

In our experience with the Deserted Island technique most clients are able to see how rigid beliefs and rules lead to a greater emotional disturbance than more flexible rules. The technique also highlights how the beliefs largely contribute to a person's level of distress and not necessarily the situation itself. This is helped by asking the client to put their problem on temporary hold and using an example in which they are not emotionally involved so that they can stand back from it and examine the effect of cognitions upon emotion.

It is important to ensure that the client has understood the model, otherwise he or she will not understand why later the therapist is devoting time to examining and questioning his unhelpful beliefs. It is good practice to obtain feedback by asking the client to explain what the example demonstrated. Once the therapist has ensured that the client has understood the model, the next step is to assess the client's negative automatic thoughts or unhelpful beliefs. A typical transcript of the assessment procedure follows below. Closely observe the use of 'verbal economy' by the therapist when eliciting the unhelpful beliefs:

> *Therapist*: You agreed that the Deserted Island model demonstrated how the rigid rules and beliefs led to high levels of stress.
>
> *Client*: Yeah.
>
> *Therapist*: Now, if we return to your problem of giving a presentation to the board of directors, what do you think you are telling yourself to add pressure to an already difficult situation? [*Therapist eliciting rigid rule or unhelpful belief.*]
>
> *Client*: I must perform well.
>
> *Therapist*: And if you don't perform well, what would be the outcome? [*Therapist assessing predicted outcome.*]
>
> *Client*: It would be awful, absolutely terrible! [*An example of magnification and catastrophizing.*]
>
> *Therapist*: Could you still accept yourself as a person? [*Therapist checking for core belief or labelling.*]
>
> *Client*: No. I would be a total failure! [*An example of labelling – therapist makes a mental note to assess in later session to confirm whether or not this is a core belief.*]
>
> *Therapist*: As long as you tell yourself [*Therapist writes A and B details on a whiteboard*]:
>
> A – Giving a presentation.
>
> B – I must perform well, and if I don't it would be awful, absolutely terrible and I would be a total failure.
>
> C – Very anxious.
>
> How will you feel?
>
> *Client*: Very anxious. [*Therapist completes ABC on whiteboard, see above.*]
>
> *Therapist*: Will that help your performance? [*Therapist checking out the behavioural consequences and reinforcing that this thinking is unhelpful and not task focused.*]
>
> *Client*: No. I get so anxious I can't think or speak properly.
>
> *Therapist*: Do you think it would be useful to examine these TICs as I call them [*therapist pointing to whiteboard*], task interfering cognitions or thoughts, and perhaps modify them to TOCs, task oriented cognitions, to help you reduce your anxiety, remain task focused and perhaps perform better?
>
> *Client*: Sounds a great idea to me.

It is important, metaphorically speaking, not to put words into the client's mouth but to help the client discover the thinking errors he or she is making when emotionally disturbed. The use of 'verbal economy' by asking short, concise assessment questions, puts the focus on to the client's thinking and avoids the therapist telling the client what he or she is thinking. This method also helps clients who are experiencing difficulty in accessing their negative automatic thoughts to discover them fairly quickly. Once the thinking errors or unhelpful beliefs have been elicited, then the therapist obtains explicit agreement from the client to examine them in further depth and, if there is sufficient time in the session, to teach the client how to question their validity. As the Deserted Island technique is usually used during the beginning stage of therapy, labelling each thinking error is strongly recommended.

Letter writing

Sometimes clients are unable to express how they feel about a particular person during a therapy session. They may be too ashamed to share their beliefs with the therapist, especially if labelling the person concerned. A useful between-session assignment is to ask the client to write a letter to the person, with a caveat that they do not send it. In many cases this leads to the client expressing what he thinks and how he feels. This is of particular use in cases of complicated grief or abuse. The therapist and client can discuss the content of the letter in the next therapy session and the relevant unhelpful beliefs can be examined. Occasionally the client may not wish to share the letter with the therapist. If this occurs then the client can be asked what benefits he derived from undertaking the exercise.

Motivation imagery

Palmer and Neenan (1998) developed a variation of time projection imagery (see Ellis et al., 1998; Lazarus, 1984) to help motivate and encourage reluctant clients to face up to and deal with their problems (see Milner and Palmer, 1998; Neenan and Palmer, 1998).

Initially, clients are asked to visualize their future based on avoiding their problem(s). This 'inaction imagery' would include all the associated disadvantages. Then they are asked to contrast this picture with another view of their future based on dealing with their problem(s). This 'action imagery' would include all the possible associated advantages. This is illustrated in the example below (adapted Palmer and Neenan, 1998: 89–91):

> Client: I really can't stand the thought of going back to work. I get too stressed out. I can't see me giving it a go.
> Therapist: It may be an good idea if we just spent a few moments considering what the rest of your life could be like if you don't return to work and overcome your fears. Is that okay?
> Client: Yeah.
> Therapist: Just imagine that after you leave here today, you go home and tell your wife that you've had enough of work. You start to discuss your future

with her. Can you see this happening in your mind's eye? [*Therapist obtaining client feedback to ensure that he is able to build up a picture.*]

Client: Easily!

Therapist: Tell me, what are some of your predictions?

Client: Well, for a start, she won't be happy. She doesn't think it's right for me to stay at home by myself whilst she's out working.

Therapist: Any other difficulties?

Client: I won't have any money I could spend on myself or my family.

Therapist: What are the sort of things you like to spend your money on?

Client: Things for the kids and my wife, CDs, beer, cigarettes, clothes, and of course, my car. I wouldn't be able to afford the road tax let alone the petrol!

Therapist: What about decorating the house or purchasing new furniture?

Client: No chance!

Therapist: Now really start to imagine this picture you are building up. You may find this exercise easier if you close your eyes. Just imagine your wife is unhappy. In fact she's started to moan at you every day. No luxuries for your children, few Christmas presents for them, no CDs, restricted beer and cigarettes, lack of decent clothes, having to wear your old jeans, and of course, no car. Can you see yourself having to use public transport; waiting for the bus on a cold, wet miserable day? [*Therapist helping the client to see the disadvantages of not facing his fears.*]

Client: Yes.

Therapist: Now imagine this situation goes on for the rest of your life. Day after day of staying at home with little funds. Can you envision this happening?

Client: Yeah. All too clearly!

Therapist: [*humorously*] I wonder if your wife would stay with you?

Client: After what she has said recently, I doubt it.

Therapist: I wonder what will happen to your confidence?

Client: What confidence!

Therapist: This situation continues until the day you die. As you see your life unfolding before you, what are your thoughts and how do you feel?

Client: Awful. What a depressing thought. The rest of my life like this. I can't see my friends wanting to visit me in this state either.

Therapist: So you really don't like this possible future scenario? [*Therapist reinforcing the disadvantages of inaction.*]

Client: No chance.

Therapist: It may be an idea now to imagine a different scenario. Just picture yourself leaving here today and going home and telling your wife that you have decided to go back to work. Picture being able to face your fears at work. Think of the financial benefits. You will be able to purchase CDs again; things for the family and yourself. Back at work, once you've over-come your fears by the application of cognitive behaviour therapy, your confidence will grow, day by day. When you're 60 you won't have to travel on the buses as you will still have your own car. Your children will grow up and you may have the pleasure of grandchildren. How do you feel now? [*Therapist reinforcing the benefits of dealing with the problem.*]

Client: A lot better.

Therapist: What do you think the purpose of this exercise was for? [*Therapist obtaining feedback.*]

Client: To show me if I don't get off my butt, my life could become more miserable than it is now. That would be terrible.
Therapist: Okay. So what options have you got?
Client: Not many! I either stay at home and get worse or go back to work.
Therapist: That's where I come in. One of my jobs is to help you to focus on examining your unhelpful demotivating beliefs and consider whether you could take a different, more motivating attitude to your current problem.

This imaginal technique is useful when clients are not prepared to face their fears or are not sufficiently motivated. This technique has also proved effective in helping clients who are in a pre-contemplative stage of therapy (i.e. reluctant to acknowledge one's problems). The client is still left with the choice of either action, inaction or, in some cases, partial action. It is important to undertake the inaction imagery first and then the action imagery, otherwise clients can be left feeling demotivated and mildly depressed. The method may be contraindicated with clients experiencing suicidal ideation or severe depression (see Palmer and Dryden, 1995 for indications and contraindications of imagery techniques). The technique is also known the 'Double Imagery Procedure' or 'Inaction versus Action Imagery' (Palmer and Neenan, 1998).

Positive imagery

To enhance a state of relaxation, in this technique a client visualizes a scene, real or imaginary, that he finds positive or pleasant. It is important to discuss with the client exactly what he finds pleasant about his scene. When the technique is initially carried out, the therapist can help reinforce the visualization by asking him to focus on different aspects of it. Clients are encouraged regularly to use this technique as it can help to inhibit or reduce anxiety and physical tension levels. As it is a good cognitive distraction technique, it is particularly useful in pain management. It can also help to counter mild depression or boredom.

Rational-emotive imagery

This technique is taken from rational emotive behaviour therapy. Although there are a number of versions, we will describe the earlier version which can be easily integrated within cognitive behaviour therapy (also see Ellis, 1979). In Maultsby's version (1975) the client is instructed to imagine a feared situation and simultaneously repeats very forcefully to herself (either aloud or internally depending upon the situation) a previously negotiated helpful coping statement. This helps clients to experience less anxiety and prepares them for difficult situations or it can be used to help them deal with how they behaved in an earlier situation. In the latter case the client's goal may be to feel less guilt or shame. It is important for the client to practise the technique initially during the session to ensure that the targeted emotion feels less intense. Rating the strength of the emotion before, during and after the exercise helps the therapist to assess whether an appropriate coping statement was chosen. If the rating stays the same throughout the exercise, then the coping statement may need altering.

Step-up technique

This technique is used if a client is anxious about a probable future event occurring such as not reaching a deadline and the underlying beliefs have been difficult to determine (see Lazarus, 1984: 25). The client is instructed to imagine the feared situation unfolding. Often this will be sufficient for the client to grasp the underlying cause of the anxiety. In some cases it is useful to ask the client to 'step-up' the scene by visualizing the very worst possible outcome. Then the client and therapist consider how the situation could be dealt with and subsequently the client is asked to repeat the exercise incorporating the new coping strategies developed. Often the client realizes that his or her very worst fear is unlikely to occur and if it did happen then it is still survivable.

Time projection imagery

Time projection imagery guides a client backwards or forwards in time to relive past events or to see that a present negative event has been overcome sometime in the future (Lazarus, 1989). For example, a client may be depressed about being made redundant. She is asked to imagine herself six months into the future and to describe what she is doing. This exercise is repeated for one year, two years and possibly five years into the future. Usually the job loss becomes less important in the future and this technique demonstrates to the client that she will be able to survive the current situation. In this scenario most clients can visualize themselves obtaining another job sometime in the future. With loss of a partner, the majority of clients foresee themselves starting new relationships, although this may be a year or two in the future. In these examples, if the client was not able to see a positive future then the therapist could ask her to imagine either being offered a new job or meeting new people, undertaking favourite pastimes, etc. This procedure generally helps to lift the client's mood and instil a sense of hope. 'Time tripping' backwards can allow the client to relive past events and put them into perspective.

Thought stopping

In the beginning stage of therapy clients may experience difficulty stopping or controlling thoughts or images about which they feel very anxious. If other methods such as audioloop taping do not appear to help, then thought stopping may be necessary. In the therapy session the client is asked to think about the obsessive thought or image (Salkovskis and Kirk, 1989). Once the client has invoked it the therapist makes a loud noise such as clapping her hands or shouting 'STOP' and also directs the client to perform the same action. Assuming that this procedure helps to stop the unwanted thought, the technique is repeated at a reduced volume until the client is able to stop the thought without having to make any external noise. This procedure is practised in the therapy session a number of times before the client undertakes the exercise as a between-session assignment.

One useful technique involves the client wearing an elastic band around his wrist and snapping it when the thought occurs. The pain distracts the client from his negative train of thought or disturbing image. Other methods of thought stopping include the client imagining a road stop sign, a red traffic light or a relaxing scene (Lazarus, 1989).

Verbal economy

In brief therapy 'time is a critical element and brevity is the watchword' (Lazarus and Fay, 1990: 43). Hoyt (1989) suggests that therapists should seize the moment. If brief therapists take these ideas seriously then it is important that they use 'verbal economy'; in other words, use the minimum number of words or phrases to convey a message, teach an idea, develop a cognitive formulation, examine and question beliefs, etc. To encourage this skill it is recommended that therapists tape-record their work and then in supervision listen to their therapy sessions and decide how they could have been more efficient (see p. 116 for an example of verbal economy).

BEHAVIOURAL INTERVENTIONS

Contracting

With this intervention the client makes a formal agreement or contracts with a significant other such as a family member or work colleague to make specific positive behavioural change that they both aspire to such as stop moaning, stop smoking or maintaining a diet (Marks, 1986). It is important that the target behaviours are not complex, are easy to repeat and viewed as positive by both parties. It is useful for both parties to write down the agreed behaviours in terms that are clear and specific. The therapist emphasizes that both parties should work together as a team and remind each other of the benefits of change.

Cost-benefit analysis of behaviours or habits

Similar to the cost-benefit analysis of beliefs, with this method the therapist helps the client to assess the pros and cons of maintaining a particular behaviour or habit that she wishes to alter. To aid this process the client notes on Form 1 (Appendix 9) the behaviour that is targeted for change. The advantages and disadvantages of continuing the behaviour or habit are noted in the relevant columns. Then on Form 2 (Appendix 10) the new desired behaviour is noted down and the advantages and disadvantages are noted in the relevant columns. This two-stage method helps clients to focus on the benefits of change. This method has also been used by experienced therapists to help clients with suicidal ideation to decide not to commit suicide.

Cue exposure

The client is exposed to the 'temptation' or cue to enable the acquisition of different methods of coping with the resultant impulsive urges. Milner and Palmer (1998) provide the example of a binge eater who may sit in front of a plate of favourite food such as biscuits and attempt to resist the urge to eat them. Eventually the urge subsides. Whenever possible, the technique should first be used in a therapy session enabling the therapist to help the client develop coping strategies to deal with the cue. It is useful for the client in the session to rate on a scale of 0–10 the strength of their urge. In the previous example the coping strategies could include cognitive distraction, aversive imagery, coping statements and relaxation techniques. Extreme care needs to be taken with clients coming off drugs in case they are tempted to lapse when alone.

Habit control

Habit control interventions are designed to reduce or stop undesired habits such as bed wetting, hair pulling, nail biting, stuttering, tics, etc. For example, clients who pull or twist their hair would be asked to clench their fists or grasp an object when they had the urge to pull. Creativity by the therapist and client is often required to develop a suitable intervention to help control the habit. Sometimes external equipment may be required; for example, when helping a child to stop bed wetting biofeedback monitors may be necessary.

Modelling

Before a client undertakes an agreed task or exercise, the therapist demonstrates or 'models' the desired behaviour in small manageable steps. It is recommended that the therapist emulates the client by demonstrating the particular skill at an acceptable standard and not in a 'perfect' manner (see Milner and Palmer, 1998; Palmer and Dryden, 1995). The client can practice the behaviour such as communication skills in the session, with the therapist giving constructive and supportive feedback. The client can then apply the skill in real life as a between-session assignment and report back on progress in the following session.

Response cost or penalty and reward

This intervention is a method of self-control training in which the client agrees to a penalty or forfeit if she does not undertake a particular behaviour (Marks, 1986). For example, a client who wishes to stop smoking agrees to donate a sum of money to his least favourite political party (excluding extreme parties) if he smokes. This technique is occasionally used when between-session assignments have been negotiated and the client has requested additional encouragement to either decrease or increase the frequency of a specific behaviour. The client usually decides upon the penalty, although initially he may need to receive some ideas from the therapist. It is useful if this intervention is paired with rewards so that when the desired behaviour occurs the client rewards himself, for example, by watching his favourite television programme.

Response prevention

Response prevention is used with clients suffering from obsessive-compulsive disorders (Salkovskis and Kirk, 1989). For this particular disorder, behavioural interventions are an essential part of the therapy programme. With this technique the client is exposed to ritual evoking cues or thoughts and she attempts to resist the urge to perform rituals. After a period of time the anxiety habituates in a similar manner to a graded exposure programme for sufferers of phobias. Homework diaries are used to monitor progress. In the early stages of therapy the client is asked to prolong the time before performing the ritual and also to reduce the number of times the ritual is performed. For example, if the client has the urge to touch an object 40 times then initially the therapist encourages the client to touch it only 30 times. For the majority of clients, if they are asked to stop touching the object completely they are likely to find this very difficult and the likelihood of attrition occurring is increased.

Self-monitoring and recording

Self-monitoring and progress recording by clients is usually very beneficial and an important part of cognitive behaviour therapy. Homework diaries and daily logs (see appendices) are particularly useful as they enable the therapist to discuss progress and any difficulties that the client may have encountered undertaking between-session assignments.

Stimulus control

Stimulus control consists of changing the environment so that the client does not have easy access to the stimulus. For example, a client who wishes to stop smoking would remove cigarettes, ashtrays and matches from his or her accommodation and temporarily would avoid visiting friends who smoked. A student who wished to focus on studying for exams would remove distractions from his or her study such as computers (especially computer games), telephones, television, etc. In addition, the student would ensure that the environment was conducive to study by having suitable lighting, desk or work surface, etc.

RELAXATION TECHNIQUES

Multimodal relaxation method

This technique was developed by Palmer (1993b) to be used in one-to-one therapy or in group settings. It provides the clients with a range of different modality interventions such as imaginal or cognitive, thereby allowing them to discover the best technique that induces a state of relaxation. Some clients prefer cognitive distractions such as mantras, whereas others prefer imagery exercises. After having tried the method then clients can either share their thoughts on the best intervention or use biofeedback galvanic skin response instruments to determine which particular modality intervention is useful. As the medical condition of group members may be unknown, muscular contraction techniques are not included as they may dangerously raise blood pressure. Deep breathing is also avoided as this can trigger panic attacks in anxious individuals (Palmer, 1992).

Clients are encouraged to choose their own image or picture to avoid the therapist inadvertently suggesting unsuitable guided images which may trigger elevated levels of anxiety or panic attacks. For example, asking a client to imagine walking through a forest may appear totally innocuous and safe. However, if that client had experienced an unpleasant or frightening incident in a forest then this image is unlikely to induce a relaxed state.

It is recommended that the exercise is tape-recorded, so that the client can use the multimodal relaxation method outside the therapy session. The end of the script can be altered to help clients fall asleep if they are suffering from insomnia or disturbed sleep patterns. If the method is being used in one-to-one therapy then the therapist can enquire beforehand what image the client would like inserted into the script.

The method has been designed to last about eight to ten minutes so that busy clients are able easily to fit it into their daily routine. Depending upon the setting, it can be lengthened if required. Clients are usually encouraged to undertake the exercise while sitting on a chair so that they can transfer the skill to other situations such as the workplace or while sitting or even standing on a train. With practice, most clients will not need to close their eyes. With regular practice clients will usually be able to use the method as a rapid relaxation technique which is particularly helpful during or prior to stressful events. In fact this is one goal of conditioned relaxation training whereby clients learn to relax in response to a specific self-produced cue. Some clients find that by breathing slowing and saying in their mind the number 'one' or 'relax' on their outbreath they can quickly relax, whereas others may need to be able to focus on a relaxing image. Therefore a trial and error stage is usually necessary as the client adapts the method to her personal requirements.

As with any technique, it is important to explain to the client how relaxation works: that it switches off the stress response and activates the parasympathetic nervous system which helps the body to relax, aids digestion, reduces heart rate and blood pressure and conserves energy.

The multimodal relaxation method is adapted from Palmer (1993b: 17–23). *Pause* is about 1–3 seconds in length. *Long pause* is about 5–15 seconds. The lengths vary depending upon the time allocated to the relaxation exercise.

If you could make yourself as comfortable as possible on your chair
[*Pause*]

And if you would just like to close your eyes
[*Pause*]
As you do this exercise, if you feel any odd feelings such as tingling sensations, light headedness, or whatever, then this is quite normal. If you open your eyes then these feelings will go away. If you carry on with the relaxation exercise usually the feelings will disappear anyway
[*Pause*]
If you would like to listen to the noises outside the room first of all
[*Long pause*]
And now listen to any noises inside of the room
[*Pause*]
You may be aware of yourself breathing
[*Pause*]
These noises will come and go probably throughout this session and you can choose to let them just drift over your mind and choose to ignore them if you so wish
[*Pause*]
Now keeping your eyelids closed and without moving your head, I would like you to look upwards, your eyes closed, just look upwards
[*Long pause: NB If clients or group participants wear contact lenses then they can remove them before the exercise or not look upwards.*]
Notice the feeling of tiredness
[*Pause*]
And relaxation
[*Pause*]
In your eye muscles
[*Pause*]
Now let your eyes drop back down
[*Pause*]
Notice the tiredness and the relaxation in those muscles of your eyes
[*Pause*]
Let the feeling now travel down your face to your jaw, just relax your jaw
[*Long pause*]
Now relax your tongue
[*Pause*]
Let the feeling of relaxation slowly travel up over your face to the top of your head
[*Pause*]
To the back of your head
[*Long pause*]
Then slowly down through the neck muscles
[*Pause*]
And down to your shoulders
[*Long pause*]
Now concentrate on relaxing your shoulders, just let them drop down
[*Pause*]
Now let that feeling of relaxation now in your shoulders slowly travel down your right arm, down through the muscles, down through your elbow, down through your wrist, to your hand, right down to your fingertips
[*Long pause*]

Let the feeling of relaxation now in your shoulders slowly travel down your left arm, down through your muscles, down through your elbow, through your wrist, down to your hand, right down to your fingertips
[*Long pause*]
And let that feeling of relaxation now in your shoulders slowly travel down your chest right down to your stomach
[*Pause*]
Just concentrate now on your breathing
[*Pause*]
Notice that every time as you breathe out you feel more
[*Pause*]
And more relaxed
[*Long pause*]
Let that feeling of relaxation travel down from your shoulders right down your back
[*Long pause*]
Right down your right leg, down through the muscles, through your knee down through your ankle
[*Pause*]
To your foot, right down to your toes
[*Long pause*]
Let the feeling of relaxation now travel down your left leg
[*Pause*]
Down through the muscles, down through your knee, down through your ankle, and foot, and right down to your toes
[*Long pause*]
I'll give you a few moments now
[*Pause*]
To allow you to concentrate on any part of your body that you would like to relax even further
[*15-second pause*]
I want you to concentrate on your breathing again
[*Pause*]
Notice as you breathe out
[*Pause*]
On each out-breath you feel more and more relaxed
[*Long pause*]
I would like you in your mind to say a number of your choice. If you cannot think of a number then perhaps the number one will do
[*Pause*]
And say it every time you breath out
[*Long pause*]
This will help you to push away any unwanted thoughts you may have
[*Pause*]
Each time you breathe out just say the number in your mind
[*30-second pause. Up to 20 minutes pause here if an extended session is required. If extended then regular input from the therapist or group facilitator is needed to remind the participants to repeat the mantra 'one' or whatever number they have chosen.*]
I want you now to stop saying the number and instead picture your favourite relaxing place

[*Pause*]
I want you to concentrate
[*Pause*]
On your favourite relaxing place
[*Long pause*]
Try and see it in your mind's eye
[*Long pause*]
Look at the colours
[*Pause*]
Perhaps concentrate on one of the colours now
[*Pause*]
Maybe one of your favourite colours if it's there
[*Long pause*]
Now concentrate on any sounds or noises or the silence in your favourite relaxing place
[*Long pause*]
Now concentrate on any smells or aromas in your favourite relaxing place
[*Long pause*]
Now just imagine touching something in your favourite relaxing place
[*Long pause*]
Just imagine how it feels
[*Long pause*]
I want you now to concentrate on your breathing again
[*Pause*]
Notice once again that every time you breathe out
[*Pause*]
You feel more
[*Pause*]
And more relaxed
[*Long pause*]
Whenever you want to in the future you will be able to remember your favourite relaxing place or the breathing exercise and it will help you to relax quickly
[*Long pause*]
In a few moments' time, but not quite yet, I'm going to count to three
[*Pause*]
And you will be able to open your eyes in your own time
[*Pause*]
[*Option: go off to sleep if you so wish if recording for clients experiencing sleeping difficulties.*]
One
[*Pause*]
Two
[*Pause*]
Three
[*Pause*]
Open your eyes in your own time [*optional*].

Similar to other relaxation techniques the multimodal relaxation method is particularly indicated for clients with anxiety, classic and common migraine, colitis, essential hypertension, high blood pressure, hyperarousal disorders (e.g. PTSD), insomnia, irritable bowel syndrome, mixed tension-vascular headache, physical tension, psychosomatic disorders, tension headache and Type A behaviour. It can also help clients to control their general irritability if they are on a stop smoking programme (Palmer and Dryden, 1995). Initially, clients will need to practise this method daily as a homework assignment to gain any benefit. To monitor progress it is recommended that clients complete a Relaxation Diary (Appendix 11; Palmer, 1993b: 52) after undertaking relaxation exercises. The client can bring the diary to the following therapy session and share his or her progress or any difficulties encountered with the therapist.

Progressive relaxation

This is an earlier form of relaxation that is often referred to in the research literature and is included in this chapter as a technique which may be useful if other methods have not proved successful. Jacobson (1938) developed 'progressive relaxation' which consisted of teaching clients to tense different groups of muscles for approximately six seconds and then to relax them for a longer period. The technique was a major development in its time. However, the entire procedure took many training sessions and was very time consuming. Later, Wolpe and Lazarus (1966) refined and shortened the process. The relaxation exercise is in four sections: relaxation of arms; facial area with neck, shoulders and upper back; chest, stomach and lower back; hips, thighs and calves followed by complete body relaxation. As the technique is repetitive and due to space constraints, only the progressive relaxation of the arms will be described below:

> Settle back as comfortably as you can. Let yourself relax to the best of your ability . . . Now, as you relax like that, clench your right fist, just clench your fist tighter and tighter, and study the tension as you do so. Keep it clenched and feel the tension in your right fist, hand, forearm . . . and now relax. Let the fingers of your right hand become loose, and observe the contrast in your feelings . . . Now let yourself go and try to become more relaxed all over . . . once more, clench your right fist really tight . . . hold it, and notice the tension again . . . now let go, relax; your fingers straighten out, and you notice the difference once more . . . [and so on].

This procedure is continued for the entire arm and takes about five minutes to complete. Different parts of the body are relaxed in a similar manner. With some clients the relaxed state can be induced more speedily and many of the instructions can be omitted. The technique is particularly useful for physically tense clients. It is indicated for clients suffering from anxiety (specific or generalized),

asthma, convulsive tic, depression, oesophageal spasm, high blood
pressure, hypertension, insomnia, pain (chronic), phobias, spasmodic
dysmenorrhoea, tension headache and tinnitus (see McGuigan,
1993). As this technique could temporarily raise blood pressure, care
should be taken with clients with cardiac disorders or glaucoma.

Relaxation response

Benson (1976) developed the relaxation response which is a western-
ized version of meditation. He removed any cultural influence and
replaced the mantra with the number 'one'. One advantage of this
technique is that the repetition of the number 'one' helps clients to
disregard any negative or distracting thoughts which occur as they
attempt to relax. Palmer and Dryden (adapted, 1995: 133) modified
the original text:

1 Find a comfortable position and sit quietly.
2 Close your eyes.
3 Relax your muscles, starting at your face and progress down to
   your toes.
4 Now concentrate on your breathing. Breathe naturally through
   your nose. In your mind say the number 'one' as you breathe
   out.
5 If negative or distracting thoughts occur, let them just pass over
   your mind and return to repeating the number 'one'. Do not try
   to force relaxation. Just let it occur in its own time.
6 Continue this exercise for a further 10–20 minutes.
7 When you finish, keep your eyes closed for a couple of minutes
   and sit quietly.

Carrington (1993: 150–1) has suggested a number of primary indications for modern forms of meditation: abuse of 'soft' drugs, alcohol
or tobacco; chronic fatigue states; chronic low-grade depressions;
difficulties with self-assertion; subacute reaction depressions; self-
blame; hypersomnias; irritability; pathological bereavement reactions
and separation anxiety; shifting emphasis from client's reliance on
therapist to reliance on self (particularly useful when terminating
therapy). Carrington (1993) warns that some clients may not be able
to tolerate the usual 20-minute sessions and in these cases the meditation time needs to be reduced.

Practice points

1 Select techniques that fit the cognitive formulation; avoid using
   techniques in a random manner.

2   Provide clients with a clear explanation of how the technique will help deal with their particular problems.
3   Obtain client feedback to ensure that they understand the purpose of the intervention.
4   When undertaking a relaxation or imagery exercise, record the session so that the client can listen to the tape as a homework assignment.
5   Use verbal economy whenever possible.

8

Hyponosis as an Adjunct to Cognitive Behaviour Therapy

Occasionally clients request hypnosis instead of cognitive behaviour therapy. It is likely that many therapists would have either referred the client elsewhere or would have attempted to persuade an existing client that cognitive behaviour therapy or one of the other forms of cognitive behaviour therapy would be equally effective (Ellis, 1986). However, the latter approach can increase the rate of attrition, that is, early termination of therapy as the client is not obtaining what they wish. Clearly, if this occurs then the client is not going to benefit from cognitive behaviour therapy. Therefore, somewhat reluctantly, this chapter has been included in the book.

When clients have a strong belief that hypnosis will help them handle difficult situations, reduce anxiety, stress, depression or overcome somatic problems, unless hypnosis is contraindicated it has been found to be a particularly useful intervention (see Kirsch et al., 1995, 1999; Lazarus, 1973, 1999; Palmer, 1993b). Hypnosis has also been recommended as a technique that can be used within a cognitive behaviour and rational emotive behaviour therapy framework, although it does have limitations (Ellis et al., 1998).

Brief cognitive behaviour therapy will, when necessary, flexibly incorporate techniques taken from a range of different therapies to enhance therapeutic outcome if they are shown to be effective, not contraindicated and preferably reinforce how beliefs affect our emotions. Therefore therapists may seriously wish to consider using hypnosis as an adjunct to cognitive behaviour therapy with clients having a strong desire to use the technique who would otherwise terminate therapy. This chapter gives an example of a hypnosis script and provides information about the different stages of traditional hypnosis. Because in cognitive behaviour therapy an open, collaborative approach is used in which the theory and practice of each intervention are explained to the client, direct suggestion explicitly focusing on the particular problem concerned is employed in the hypnosis script and indirect suggestion is avoided.

Hypnosis script

In this section a typical hypnosis script is described and, for convenience, has been divided into the conventional hypnosis stages.

Preparation and preliminary induction
In the preparation stage, the therapist ensures that the client is put at ease. This may involve answering any questions that the client may have about hypnosis. Typical questions asked are (Palmer, 1993b):

- What is hypnosis?
- How will I know if I've been hypnotized?
- Will you take control of my mind?
- What will you be doing?
- What happens if I don't come out of hypnosis?
- Will I tell you all my secrets?

The majority of clients will have their own views of the nature of hypnosis and some even liken it to a stage act they have seen. It is important to provide a more therapeutically helpful explanation of what it is and how it works. We indicate that it can be considered as a form of relaxation where the mind is receptive to constructive helpful coping suggestions. In addition, hypnosis will only occur if clients want it to happen. They will be in control and if they want to wake up they will be able to. They will not reveal any secrets if they do not want to.

Unlike formal hypnosis, as this will be undertaken within a cognitive behaviour framework, the first session is still spent assessing the client's problem(s), in particular focusing on eliciting key thinking errors and behavioural goals for therapy. About ten minutes may be allocated to a relaxation exercise such as the multimodal relaxation method (pp. 124–9) to ensure that the client is able to relax and discover which particular modality she prefers to use. For example, some clients are more receptive to using imagery techniques to relax, whereas others prefer to use breathing techniques. Hypnosis is used during the second session.

At the preliminary induction stage, the client can be told that it is quite normal during hypnosis to feel tingling, warm or heavy feelings in their hands and limbs. It is recommended that the client either lies on a couch or is seated in a comfortable chair with a headrest. The room should be at a reasonable temperature as some clients feel cold during hypnosis (or relaxation). The therapy room preferably needs to be located in a quiet part of the building. It is usually more comfortable for clients if they remove their contact lenses or spectacles.

The preliminary induction part of the hypnosis script is designed to encourage a state of hypnoidal relaxation. Whether a 'hypnoidal' state actually exists is debatable. However, this is not relevant as client expectation that hypnosis will prove helpful is probably the most important component in effective hypnosis (see Lazarus, 1973). In the script described, unlike the more traditional methods, the therapist does not 'will' the client to close his or her eyes as this may increase resistance and be counterproductive in some cases.

Deepening

The deepening stage of hypnosis is designed to increase the depth of relaxation. The method described later in the hypnosis script uses a counting and breathing technique. This method can be used in most cases except where clients experience breathing difficulties, for example, smokers. In those cases or with clients who can easily visualize scenes, an imagery method may be preferable. If imagery deepening is selected, then a particular suitable relaxing scene would need to be elicited from the client beforehand. Imagery that involves the client imagining going down something such as a hill, a lift, flight of stairs, a beach or a country lane is ideal. At this stage it is advisable to avoid imagery that may trigger anxiety as this will not help the relaxation process; for example, instructing a client who is phobic of escalators to imagine using a escalator. If clients want to overcome a particular phobia then suitable coping imagery is focused on during the ego-strengthening part of hypnosis.

A typical imagery deepener is described below. It has been found helpful for the therapist to gently emphasize the trigger words '*DOWN*' and '*NOW*' as this seems to induce a deeper state of relaxation in clients.

Optional imagery deepener (Palmer, 1993b: 28–31)

I want you now to imagine that you are at the top of the hill that you described to me earlier
[*Pause*]
Just look at the view. Notice the colours of the plants in the fields
[*Pause*]
As you look down the hill you can see the cows in the meadow at the bottom of the hill
[*Pause*]
You can feel the warmth of the sun on your face
[*Pause*]
In a few moments' time
[*Pause*]
But not quite yet

[*Pause*]
You are going to take three steps *down* the hill, one at a time
[*Pause*]
And by the time you take the third step you will be at the bottom of the hill in the meadow
[*Pause*]
And every time you take one step *down* the hill you will feel more and more relaxed than you do *now*
[*Pause*]
In a few moments' time you are going to take your first step *down* the hill, but not quite yet, and when you do, you are going to feel so very relaxed
[*Pause*]
Take your first step *down* the hill *now*
[*Pause*]
Now you are feeling more relaxed than you did a few seconds ago, a few minutes ago, a few hours ago, a few days ago, even a few weeks ago
[*Pause*]
Now that you are one-third of the way *down* the hill, notice how your view has changed
[*Pause*]
Take your time and just look at the view that you know so well. And as you look around, notice how very relaxed you are now feeling
[*Pause*]
Can you see that you are now closer to the bottom of the hill. Your view of the meadow has improved
[*Pause*]
In a few moments' time, I'm going to ask you to take your second step *down* the hill, and when you take that step you are going to feel even more relaxed than you do *now*
[*Pause*]
Take your second step *down* the hill *now*
[*Pause*]
Now you feel even more relaxed than you did a few moments ago, a few minutes ago, much more relaxed than you did a few hours ago
[*Pause*]
Your view has altered again as you approach the bottom of the hill. The meadow looks much closer. If you look back up the hill, notice how far away the top of the hill now seems
[*Pause*]
Look in the fields at the plants and the cows. Notice the smells of the flowers in the hedgerow.
[*Pause*]
You are feeling so very relaxed now, it feels that you are really there on your favourite countryside walk
[*Pause*]
In a few moments' time, but not quite yet, you take your last step *down* the hill, and when you do, you will feel so very relaxed when you arrive in the meadow
[*Pause*]
Take your last step *down* the hill *now*
[*Pause*]

Now you are feeling so very, very relaxed. More relaxed than you felt a few moments ago, a few minutes ago, much more relaxed than you felt a few hours ago

[*At this point, continue with the ego-strengthening script.*]

Ego strengthening

This is the key part of the process where the therapist modifies the previously assessed thinking errors and unhelpful beliefs and behaviours and inserts powerful coping statements to directly counter them (see Palmer, 1997b). The script can be altered to take into account any general condition from which the client may be suffering such as migraines, etc. It is also useful to reiterate the positive effects of hypnosis outside the therapeutic hour (Palmer, 1993b). This may have a beneficial post-hypnotic effect which is an important component of hypnosis.

Coping imagery can be included to help the client to deal with difficult situations such as giving presentations or dealing with phobias (Palmer and Dryden, 1995). Rational-emotive imagery can be used to demonstrate that clients can stand difficult situations and events. Forward time projection imagery can be used to highlight that the client can stand current adverse situations and that events are seldom 'terrible' indefinitely (Lazarus, 1984; Palmer and Dryden, 1995). However, it is important to select the appropriate imagery technique for a specific problem.

In the script, the 'pauses' help to underscore the ego-strengthening suggestions and enhance their effect (Palmer, 1993b).

Symptom removal

The symptom removal stage is used if the client is experiencing difficulty dealing with a particular psychosomatic or physical symptom. If this stage is left out, then the termination script can be inserted at this point. Symptom removal is targeted at specific symptoms from which the client may be suffering such as allergies, anxiety, asthma, habits (e.g. overeating, smoking), headaches, insomnia, migraine, pain, panic attacks, phobias, tics, skin disorders, speech disorders, etc. (see Palmer, 1993b). The script illustrated in the text may help with the alleviation of migraine and tension headaches. Hartland (1971) can be consulted for a wide range of symptom removal scripts.

It is important when dealing with clients with so-called symptoms of stress or physical pains to ensure that the client does not have an underlying organic condition. An appropriate referral to a medical practitioner may be necessary.

Termination
The termination stage is the last part of the hypnosis procedure. If clients open their eyes before the hypnosis script has been completed then they are asked to close their eyes and the termination stage is executed.

Debrief
It is helpful to discover what the client thought and felt about the experience and to answer any queries that may have arisen during the session. If the client wants to receive hypnosis again in a later session then it is useful to ask whether he or she would like any part of the script altered.

Hyponosis script

Preliminary induction (adapted Palmer, 1993b: 33–6)
   Can you make yourself as comfortable as possible in your chair
   [*Pause*]
   And if you would just like to close your eyes
   [*Pause*]
   If you would like to listen to the noises outside the room
   [*Pause*]
   And now listen to the noises inside the room
   [*Pause*]
   These noises will come and go probably throughout this session and you can choose to let them just drift over your mind and choose to ignore them if you so wish
   [*Pause*]
   You will probably notice how these noises and the sound of my voice will become softer and louder and softer again during this session. This is quite normal and will indicate that you are in a state of hypnosis
   [*Pause*]
   Let your whole body go limp and slack
   [*Pause*]
   Now keeping your eyelids closed and without moving your head, I would like you to look upwards, keep your eyes closed, just look upwards
   [*Pause*]
   Notice the feeling of tiredness, sleepiness
   [*Pause*]
   And relaxation
   [*Pause*]
   In your eye muscles
   [*Pause*]
   And when your eyes feel so tired, so very, very, tired, just let your eyes drop back *down*
   [*Pause*]

Notice the feeling of tiredness, sleepiness and relaxation in your eyes
[*Pause*]
Let this travel *down* your face to your jaw
[*Pause*]
Now just relax your jaw
[*Pause*]
If your teeth are clenched, then unclench them
[*Pause*]
Now relax your tongue. If it's touching the roof of your mouth then just let it fall down
[*Pause*]
Let the feeling of relaxation slowly travel up over your face to your forehead
[*Pause*]
To the top of your head
[*Pause*]
To the back of your head
[*Long pause*]
Then slowly *down* through the neck muscles
[*Pause*]
and *down* to your shoulders
[*Long pause*]
Now concentrate on relaxing your shoulders, just let them drop *down*
[*Pause*]
Now let that feeling of relaxation in your shoulders slowly travel *down* your right arm, *down* through the muscles, *down* through your elbow, *down* through your waist, *down* to your hand, right *down* to your fingertips
[*Long pause*]
Now let that feeling of relaxation in your shoulders slowly travel *down* your left arm, *down* through the muscles, *down* through your elbow, *down* through your wrist, *down* to your hand, right *down* to your fingertips
[*Long pause*]
And let that feeling of relaxation in your shoulders slowly travel *down* your chest right *down* to your stomach
[*Pause*]
Notice that every time you breathe out, you feel more and more relaxed.
[*Pause*]
Let that feeling of relaxation and tiredness travel *down* from your shoulders *down* your back, right *down* through your back muscles
[*Long pause*]
Right *down* your right leg, *down* through the muscles, *down* through your knee, *down* through your ankle
[*Pause*]
To your foot, right *down* to your toes
[*Long pause*]
Let the feeling of relaxation and tiredness now travel *down* your left leg
[*Pause*]
Down through the muscles, *down* through your knee, *down* through your ankle
[*Pause*]
To your foot, right *down* to your toes
[*Long pause*]

I'll give you a few moments now
[*Pause*]
To allow you to concentrate on any part of your body that you would like to relax even further
[*15-second pause or longer if necessary.*]

Deepening (adapted Palmer, 1993b: 36–8)

I want you now to concentrate on your breathing
[*Pause*]
Notice how every time you breathe out, you feel more and more relaxed
[*Pause*]
With each breath you take you feel so relaxed, so very, very relaxed
[*Pause*]
Breathe in slowly through your nose and slowly out through your mouth
[*Pause*]
With each breath you take
[*Pause*]
Every time you take a new breath of air
[*Pause*]
You are becoming more and more relaxed
[*Pause*]
Gradually you are drifting away as you become more and more relaxed
[*Pause*]
On every out-breath you are becoming more and more sleepy
[*Pause*]
More and more deeply relaxed
[*Pause*]
Notice how, as you relax, you are breathing more and more slowly
[*Pause*]
And more, and more, steadily, as you become more, and more, deeply, very deeply, relaxed
[*Pause*]
You are drifting *down* into a deep state of relaxation
[*Pause*]
Your whole body is becoming more and more relaxed, every time you breathe out
[*Pause*]
I'm slowly going to count to five, and as I do, you will feel even more relaxed than you do now
[*Pause*]
One
[*Pause*]
Now you are feeling more and more relaxed than you did a few minutes ago. More and more relaxed than you did a few seconds ago
[*Pause*]
Two
[*Pause*]
Notice how you are feeling so relaxed that you are finding it so difficult to concentrate on my voice all the time
[*Pause*]

Three
[*Pause*]
Now every time I say a number, every time you breathe out, you feel more and more deeply, very, very deeply relaxed. An overwhelming feeling of tiredness and relaxation is descending upon you as you listen to my voice
[*Pause*]
Four
You are feeling even more relaxed *now* than you did a few minutes, a few seconds ago. In a moment when I say the number five, but not quite yet, you are going to feel so very deeply relaxed
[*Pause*]
Five
[*Pause*]
Now you feel even more relaxed than you did a moment ago, more relaxed than a few seconds ago, much more relaxed than you did a few minutes ago, and very much more relaxed than you did a few hours ago.
[*Pause*]

Ego-strengthening (adapted Palmer, 1993b: 38–41)

You are now so relaxed, so very relaxed, that you are becoming very aware of what I am saying to you
[*Pause*]
You are so aware that your mind is open to any positive suggestions I may make for your benefit
[*Pause*]
You are feeling so relaxed that when I make positive suggestions about your health, you will accept these suggestions, and gradually over a period of time you will feel better and better, even though you will not be here with me
[*Pause*]
My suggestions will just drift over your mind and you will be able to remember all the relevant ones that will influence your feelings
[*Pause*]
Your thoughts
[*Pause*]
And your behaviour
[*Pause*]
As you feel more and more deeply relaxed during this session, you will find new energy to help you cope with any problems you may have had recently
[*Pause*]
New energy to lessen any fatigue
[*Pause*]
New energy to help you concentrate on your goals
[*Pause*]
A new strength of mind and body to deal with internal and external pressures
[*Pause*]
Gradually, you will become absorbed in life again, looking forward to every day
[*Pause*]
And as every day goes by, you will become more relaxed, and much calmer than you have been for some time

[*Pause*]

And each day, you will feel far less tense, and far less concerned with unimportant matters

[*Pause*]

And as this happens, your confidence will grow as your old fears become a distant memory

[*Pause*]

Week by week, day by day, hour by hour, minute by minute, second by second, your independence will grow

[*Pause*]

Any anxiety or depression or guilt or stress will fade away as you learn to cope with life

[*NB Target relevant emotion or physical state according to the client's presenting problem.*]

[*Pause*]

You will be able to stand difficult situations much more easily

[*Pause*]

You will no longer hear yourself saying 'I can't stand it', but instead you will realistically say to yourself, 'It's unpleasant but *I can stand it*'

[*Pause*]

As you learn that you can stand situations, you will procrastinate less often and you will be able to start and continue your tasks more easily

[*Pause*]

You will question whether things are really terrible. They may be bad but are they really terrible?

[*Pause*]

As you realize that you can stand situations, and that things are seldom, if ever, terrible, you will be able to face your fears much more easily

[*Pause*]

If you fail at a task, you will not condemn yourself as a total failure or stupid

[*Pause*]

All it means is that you did not achieve your target

[*Pause*]

No more, no less

[*Pause*]

You will learn to accept yourself more for the person you are and not just for your achievements

[*Pause*]

Your internal rules and demands, many of those unnecessary, inflexible musts and shoulds

[*Pause*]

Will change to preferences and coulds and subsequently your anxieties will lessen

[*Target relevant emotion according to the client's presenting problem.*]

[*Pause*]

Gradually, as time goes by, you will feel better and better and your life will improve

[*Pause*]

And your recent worries will be a thing of the past

[*Pause*]

And you will be able to put them behind you
[*Pause*]

An example of symptom removal (adapted Palmer, 1993b: 42–3)

Day by day, week by week, month by month
[*Pause*]
As you become much more relaxed
[*Pause*]
And far less tense
[*Pause*]
Gradually, the tension in your shoulders
[*Pause*]
And in your neck will fade
[*Pause*]
You will stand and sit in a very relaxed manner
[*Pause*]
And as you do, you will feel so comfortable that any pain will become a distant memory
[*Pause*]
If you concentrate now on your face
[*Pause*]
On your head
[*Pause*]
And on your neck, notice how, as you relax even further
[*Pause*]
Gradually your head and face are starting to feel warm
[*Pause*]
As this feeling of warmth increases, you are starting to feel even more relaxed than you did a few minutes ago
[*Pause*]
And day by day
[*Pause*]
As you feel less tense, in your body and mind, this state of relaxation will help to prevent headaches occurring
[*Pause*]
And as the pain is normally related to stress and tension
[*Pause*]
Day by day, as you become more relaxed
[*Pause*]
And less tense, the pain will diminish
[*Pause*]
And if you ever feel the headache returning
[*Pause*]
You will be able to sit down, relax your shoulders
[*Pause*]
Relax your neck muscles
[*Pause*]
Relax your face and head
[*Pause*]

And the pain will just drift away
[*Pause*]

Termination (adapted Palmer, 1993b: 43–4)
In a few moments' time, but not quite yet, I am going to count to three, and
when I do, you will open your eyes and wake up, and feel relaxed and
refreshed
[*Pause*]
You will be able to remember or forget whatever you want to of this hypnosis
session
And you will be in full control of your body and mind
[*Pause*]
And wake up today on [*insert here: day, time, location*]
[*Pause*]
As I count to three, you will wake up
[*NB Therapist starts to speak louder with each subsequent number*]
[*Pause*]
One
[*Pause*]
Two
[*Pause*]
Three
[*Pause*]
Open your eyes in your own time.

Comments

Albert Ellis who originated rational emotive behaviour therapy, has
found that the depth of the trance achieved by his clients made little
difference to the effectiveness of hypnosis. Therefore a deep trance
state may be unnecessary and in some cases counterproductive if the
client does not concentrate on the ego strengthening stage. It is
recommended that clients record the hypnosis session and regularly
listen to the tape at home. Ellis encourages clients to listen to the tapes
on a daily basis for one or two months to enable the REBT messages
to get through (Ellis, 1986, 1993). Ellis often only uses hypnosis for a
single session. Wherever possible, Ellis prefers not to use hypnosis at
all, but will use it as an adjunct to therapy if necessary.

Indications and contraindications
Hypnosis is indicated for psychosomatic and stress-related disorders,
anger, anxiety, asthma, allergies, behavioural problems (e.g. smoking,
tics, overeating and weight control), blushing, common and classic
migraine, depression, guilt, hurt, hypertension, insomnia, irritable
bowel syndrome, pain, phobias, physical tension, shame, skin disorders (e.g. eczema), stress, speech disorders (e.g. stammering) and

tension headache (see Hartland, 1971; Kirsch, et al., 1995, 1999; Palmer, 1993b; Palmer and Dryden, 1995).

Hypnosis has been used since the turn of the century, if not longer, for 'shell shock' or 'traumatic neurosis' (see Edgell, 1926; Pfister, 1917). These conditions are now commonly known as post-traumatic stress disorder (PTSD). However, research indicates that hypnosis may not be the intervention of choice for PTSD as cognitive restructuring by itself or combined with exposure is more effective (see review in Penava et al., 1995). Interestingly, supportive therapy is the least effective intervention whereas brief psychodynamic therapy is on a par with hypnosis. More research is needed in this area because it is possible that if the hypnosis included imaginal exposure/implosion and cognitive restructuring methods, then the technique would be more effective. A similar but less directive method has been discussed elsewhere (Moore, 1993).

Palmer and Dryden (1995) caution against using hypnosis if the client is under the influence of drugs or alcohol. Generally hypnosis is contraindicated in clients suffering from severe psychiatric disorders, although this has been challenged (see Gafner and Young, 1998; Spiegel, 1983). It is not recommended for hysterical and conversion reaction symptoms unless the client is also receiving therapy to resolve any underlying conflicts. Palmer and Dryden also suggest that care needs to be taken when using hypnosis with clients who suffer from asthma, epilepsy or narcolepsy as hypnosis (or other forms of relaxation) may in rare cases exacerbate the condition.

Conclusion

Hypnosis as a therapeutic adjunct to cognitive behaviour therapy has been found beneficial for many individuals (Kirsch et al., 1999) although it does suffer from some shortcomings. Depending upon how it is applied, the key disadvantages (Palmer, 1997b) are:

1   Hypnosis is not considered an elegant intervention from a cognitive behaviour therapy perspective as the client is not directly involved in examining the validity of his or her unhelpful beliefs.
2   Hypnosis does not necessarily help clients to restructive beliefs for themselves.
3   Hypnosis can encourage magical thinking.
4   Hypnosis may reinforce the notion that change should be easy, etc.
5   Hypnosis may discourage hard work and practice outside the therapy session.

However, as brief cognitive behaviour therapy is concerned with the efficient use of a limited number of sessions in order to produce a therapeutically optimum outcome, then hypnosis may be beneficial for a percentage of clients.

Practice points

1   When a client requests hypnosis, decide whether the intervention as an adjunct to brief cognitive behaviour therapy or as a cognitive intervention by itself would be beneficial.
2   Prepare the client for hypnosis and provide a rationale for how the intervention works at a cognitive and behavioural level; i.e. helps the client to be receptive to helpful coping strategies.
3   Ensure that the thinking errors and unhelpful beliefs are assessed before using hypnosis.
4   Negotiate helpful alternatives that counter the thinking errors and unhelpful beliefs.
5   Discuss the possible benefits of introducing coping or time projection imagery focusing on dealing with the client's problem(s) into the script.
6   Record the session so that the client can listen to the tape daily.

9

Treatment Protocols

In our whistlestop tour of cognitive behaviour therapy, we noted that this particular form of therapy had been most comprehensively applied to depression. Some recommendations in applying cognitive behaviour therapy to depression and other types of specific problems are given below. These recommendations are used in conjunction with the processes and techniques of cognitive behaviour therapy outlined throughout this book and cannot be considered separately. We have included a section on suicide as this always merits particular attention and action from the therapist when present (and its presence may be masked). The presence of suicidal ideation so often leads to considerable anxieties in trainee therapists.

Panic disorder

- For further information see Barlow and Craske (1989); Beck (1987); Beck et al. (1985); Clark (1986); Hackman (1998); Salkovskis (1988); Salkovskis et al. (1991); Wells (1997).
- See client weekly.
- Work together with client to produce a hypothesis about his negative thoughts which is then tested out.
- Main aim of treatment is to modify client's catastrophic interpretations of bodily sensations.
- Use behavioural experiments to reproduce and reduce symptoms, for example, voluntary hyperventilation exercises in session.
- Generate alternative, non-catastrophic interpretations, by use of education and/or thought challenging.
- Test out the validity of catastrophic and non-catastrophic interpretations by discussion (socratic dialogue) and behavioural experiments.
- Reproduce panic sensations within therapy and test out the consequences within therapy.
- Work with client to drop safety behaviours.
- Use relaxation training (Bernstein and Borkovec, 1973; Goldfried and Davison, 1976; Jacobson, 1938; Ost, 1987; Palmer, 1993b). See Chapter 7 for script.

Social phobia

- For further information see Beck et al. (1985); Liebowitz et al. (1985); Lucock and Salkovskis (1988); Mattick and Peters (1988); Mattick et al. (1989); Ost et al. (1981); Wells (1997, 1998).
- Teach the client about the effects of anxiety and panic.
- Teach applied relaxation, which combines exposure with training in relaxation where symptoms are mainly physiological.
- Teach hyperventilation control (Salkovskis et al., 1986).
- Introduce client to cognitive behaviour therapy model of social phobia – explore underlying fears of negative evaluation.
- Client's initial predictions of social or performance situations overestimate the probability of a negative outcome: use hypothesis testing to check out and counter such beliefs.
- Cognitive restructuring: repeatedly identify and challenge specific thoughts which drive the client's social phobia.
- Identify common thinking errors, examine and question.
- Encourage client exposure to situations in which negative evaluations could occur to allow worst fears to be disconfirmed. Therapist preparation is essential. Exposure to a range of situations is often more helpful.
- Where symptoms are predominantly behavioural use purely behavioural treatments.
- Teach assertiveness skills.
- Devise home assignments.

Generalized anxiety disorder

- For further information see Andrews et al. (1992); Butler and Booth (1991); Butler et al. (1991); Durham and Allan (1993); Hunt and Singh (1991); Wells (1997).
- Discuss goals for treatment with client at start of therapy, matching therapist and client goals for therapy.
- Give rationale for treatment and information about the disorder including anxiety management, cognitive behaviour therapy and graded exposure.
- Convey the message that changes in long-standing patterns of thinking and behaviour are possible, but point out that years of habitual thinking and behaving will not change overnight.
- Empower clients to take responsibility for changes in their own behaviour and to recognize the need to practise the skills they are taught.
- Teach the client realistically to assess the reality of danger.
- Give rationale for the elimination of reassurance seeking.

- Monitor reassurance seeking outside sessions.
- Emphasize that regular homework is important.
- Use formulation of client's problems to help her understand her symptoms and to give clarity to the cognitive behaviour therapy framework.
- Teach methods of relaxation and discuss its importance.
- Help the client to recognize tension.
- Help her to identify and deal with unrealistic thinking and worry.
- Introduce distraction techniques.
- Build up coping strategies to deal with threatening situations.
- Focus on any avoidances and give rationale.
- Focus on graded exposure programme – use imaginal exposure for rehearsal.
- Introduce problem-solving techniques.

Depression

- For further information see Abramson et al. (1978); Beck (1967, 1976); Beck et al. (1979); Fennell and Teasdale (1987); Lewinsohn et al. (1982); Rehm (1982); Scott (1998).
- Encourage acceptance of depression.
- Assess current difficulties.
- Agree a problem list.
- Define goals.
- Assess for hopelessness and suicidal thoughts during the initial session and establish the seriousness of such thoughts.
- Ask questions and gather information on whether or not plans have been made to commit suicide, how well thought through they are and what prevents the client from carrying them out. For more information on suicide see the final section in this chapter.
- Monitor client's mood.
- Explain the cognitive model.
- Develop cognitive conceptualization.
- Teach activity scheduling of pleasure and achievement: rate each activity from 0–10.
- Identify automatic thoughts.
- Identify and counter thinking errors using experiments.
- Teach techniques for cognitive restructuring and problem solving.
- Develop coping strategies.
- Prepare for setbacks.
- Ensure lapse or relapse reduction is included.

Obsessive compulsive disorder

- For further information see Foa (1979); Foa et al. (1983a, 1983b, 1985); Salkovskis (1985); Salkovskis and Warwick (1985); Salkovskis and Westbrook (1987); Salkovskis et al. (1998); Wells (1997).
- Explain treatment rationale including graded exposure, response prevention and habituation, giving examples.
- Ensure client recognizes the importance of him taking an active part in his own treatment.
- Where intrusive thoughts with behavioural rituals are present ask him to list cues or triggers that provoke discomfort and the urge to ritualize together with the associated response to such stimuli.
- Discuss the role of anticipatory anxiety emphasizing the fact that anticipation of the encounter is often more anxiety provoking than the actual physical confrontation: demonstrate this within the treatment session.
- Examine and question unhelpful beliefs, in particular the need for certainty, control and responsibility.
- Look out for client's distraction techniques during graded exposure.
- Identify whether there are intrusive thoughts present or neutralizing responses to such thoughts.
- Rate obsessions hierarchically and request client refrain from neutralizing.
- Expose client to least anxiety engendering thoughts by using audioloop cassette tape and rate discomfort and anxiety (see Chapter 7).
- Set similar tasks as home assignments.
- As habituation takes place for each thought it may be useful to vary the tone or loudness of the tape or listen to the tape in previously avoided situations.
- Other techniques to habituation may be useful: repeated writing of the intrusive thought combined with prevention of the covert neutralizing response.
- Homework tasks are an integral part of the treatment as is self-directed response prevention.

Post-traumatic stress disorder

- For further information see Andrews et al. (1994); Barlow (1988); Foa and Kozak (1986); Foa et al. (1989); Ochberg (1996); Scott and Palmer (2000); Scott and Stradling (1992, 1998).

- Elicit coping strategies which usually involve cognitive or emotional avoidance.
- Find out if these strategies work and if so for how long.
- Teach productive coping strategies for dealing with intrusive memories.
- Manage the memory (confront the memory).
- Help unlock positive memories.
- Help client to see self apart from the trauma (non-trauma-related self) and not just as victim or survivor but a whole person with a history, prior and after the event.
- Encourage client to keep self active and to schedule uplifting things to do.
- Teach management of anger and irritability.
- Teach problem-solving techniques.
- Access the old self and the old way of functioning prior to the trauma.
- Reduce the helplessness evoked by the trauma.
- Address guilt issues.
- Rewrite the script of the trauma.
- Help reconnect with others and establish life goals; encourage talking to partner/family about the trauma.
- Establish new goals – break them down into small manageable steps.
- Focus on thinking errors – those prior to and after the trauma – and help client identify their use of them.
- Elicit core beliefs related to trauma, examine, question and develop more helpful beliefs.
- Focus on processing of emotional information, for example teach client to stop and think through the meaning of an emotion rather than engage in reactive behaviour.
- Help label and understand the client's emotional state.
- Use appropriate imagery techniques to aid processing of traumatic event.
- Exposure to relevant avoided situations.
- Encourage continuity of pre-trauma experiences.
- Teach relaxation techniques, if necessary.
- Introduce lapse or relapse reduction.

Specific phobias

- For further information, see Andrews et al. (1994); Barlow (1988); Beck et al. (1985); Foa and Kozac (1986); Marks (1986); Ost (1987); Wolpe and Lazarus (1966).

- Identify specific focus of client's fears which will be an object (for example, dog) or situation (for example, heights).
- Blood injury phobia is unique in that client may faint when exposed to trigger stimulus.
- Main aim of treatment is threefold: (a) to reduce level of anxiety when exposed to feared object or situation; (b) to reduce anticipatory anxiety; (c) to reduce avoidance of the feared object or situation.
- Thrust of treatment is mainly behavioural: client is encouraged to face feared object or situation. This is known as exposure.
- Exposure should be *challenging but not overwhelming*.
- Exposure needs to be long enough for anxiety to reduce.
- Use scales to measure anxiety levels and monitor progress: see Chapter 4.
- Actual exposure is preferable to exposure in imagination.
- Develop exposure programme in collaboration with client.
- Start exposure with the least feared object or situation and progress to the most feared (for example, from small spider to big fat hairy spider).
- Systematic desensitization uses graded exposure in imagination combined with relaxation to minimize anxiety.
- Cognitive components are the use of coping self statements, relabelling and reappraisal of the feared object or situation. This aids exposure and helps to avoid premature termination.

Single session therapy

For further information, see Ellis (1995); Ellis et al. (1998); Feltham (1997); Lazarus (1997); Marks (1989); McMullin (1986); Palmer and Dryden (1995); Talmon (1990).

Single session therapy is often requested when a client has been asked at short notice to deal with a specific task, crisis, or in some cases, face a particular situation of which they are phobic, for example, giving a presentation at work.

Prior to the therapy session inform the prospective client that therapy may last approximately between one and two hours. If possible, discover what the problem appears to be and send the client relevant cognitive behaviour bibliotherapy such as books, articles or handouts.

Unless otherwise contraindicated, encourage the client to record an audiotape of the session so that the client can listen to it outside of therapy to remind her of the application of the techniques.

Explain limitations of one therapy session, i.e. limited goals. Set agenda and note target problem(s). Be realistic, avoid attempting too much for one session.

Develop and share with the client a quick formulation which focuses on relevant unhelpful beliefs and behaviours that are associated with the target problem(s). Include the client's strengths and available resources. Note down anything that the client has found to ameliorate his or her problem(s).

Be assertive. If the client wants to discuss a range of issues remind her that there is limited time available. Ask whether discussing these other issues will help her to deal with her previously agreed target problem.

If possible, if the client is phobic, undertake in-vivo exposure during the session.

Use verbal economy. Avoid providing long winded explanations.

Approximately every 30 minutes remind the client how much time is left of the session. Maintain this focus.

Depending upon the client, decide which beliefs to focus on in the session, i.e. negative automatic thoughts, intermediate beliefs, core beliefs or a combination. If appropriate, discuss with client. Remember, one session is usually insufficient to modify core beliefs. Have realistic expectations.

Use simple and straight forward interventions and techniques that focus on key unhelpful beliefs and behaviours. Use relaxation if physiological arousal is high.

Practise relevant techniques in session to ensure that the client knows how to apply them.

If relevant use the problem-solving approach. Break down problem into manageable steps. If indicated, include coping statements, imagery exercises and relaxation.

To check whether the therapy session was useful encourage the client to give you a progress report (by letter, email or telephone).

Suicide

• For further information see Beck et al. (1974a, 1974b, 1976); Curwen (1997: 58–66); Robins et al. (1959); Roy (1982, 1992); Schneidman (1985); Symonds (1985); Weishaar and Beck (1992). Some useful questionnaires relating to suicide are as follows:

1 Reasons for living scale (Linehan, 1985) to measure adaptive characteristics in suicide.
2 Scale for suicide ideation (Beck et al., 1971).
3 Hopelessness scale (Beck et al., 1974b) to assess degree of suicide risk.
4 Prediction of suicide scale (Beck et al., 1974a).

5   Los Angeles suicide prevention scale (Los Angeles Center for Suicide Prevention, 1973).

6   Beck depression inventory (Beck, 1978).

Factors associated with increased risk

- Majority of persons who successfully commit suicide have made their intentions known to at least one other person.
- More common in men than women but the risk is increasing in young men.
- Risk increases with age and is greatest in people who are single, widowed or divorced.
- Pay special attention to thoughts (cognitions) associated with any past suicide attempt(s). A previous suicide attempt may be a predictor that suicide may be contemplated in the future.
- Pay special attention to any current suicidal impulses.
- Cognitions of hopelessness have been shown to be one of the best predictors of suicidal ideation.
- If the client strongly believes that living is an endless cycle of emotional pain and distress this may indicate that suicide is viewed as a more viable option than living.
- A precise suicide plan with a lethal method arranged for the next 24 to 48 hours constitutes a high risk. Clients will require a safe environment or hospitalization.
- Clients with a life-threatening or chronic physical illness are at greater risk, as are those who are depressed or have other psychiatric illnesses.
- Risk is also heightened for those who misuse drugs and alcohol or who are socially isolated or unemployed.

Therapeutic interventions

Any person who wishes to end their life may find a way to do so. It is important to take all messages about suicide seriously. These may be conveyed in a variety of ways and contexts: for example, behaviour such as cessation of eating or drinking; giving away personal possessions or tidying up personal affairs; written messages conveying different aspects of suicidal ideation; pictures or other symbols and verbalization of suicide-related thoughts. Do not be afraid to explore suicidal ideation with your client. This does not make suicide more likely if the guidelines are followed.

- Target thoughts of hopelessness.
- Focus on strenghtening thoughts and desires to live and weakening thoughts and urges to die.

- Teach problem-solving techniques and abilities:
  - awareness of changes in moods
  - awareness of unhelpful thoughts
  - introduce experiments (cognitive and behavioural)
  - assist the client to draw up helpful action plans as alternatives to suicide.
- Allocate time and attention to suicidal thoughts or a recent suicide attempt.
- Help clients to view life crises from a non-catastrophic perspective.
- Assist in bringing about hope for the future by helping the client to see that there are alternatives to suicide.

Practice points

1 Use the protocols alongside the general principles and practice of cognitive behaviour therapy outlined elsewhere in this book – not in isolation from them.
2 Continue to develop your knowledge of the treatment protocols from this chapter and from other sources and training.
3 Any person who wishes to end their life may find a way to do so.
4 Remain aware of the factors which have been identified for those most at risk of suicide.
5 The majority of people who commit suicide have made their intentions known to at least one other person.
6 Take all messages about suicide seriously. Do not be afraid to explore suicidal ideation with your client. This does not make suicidal behaviour more likely.
7 A previous attempt at suicide is an important predictor that suicide may be contemplated in the future.
8 Clients with an immediate, lethal and precise suicide plan will require a safe environment or hospitalization.
9 Questionnaires are helpful in assessing the suicidal potential of individuals when used in conjunction with other assessment methods.

Afterword

We have aimed to provide the reader with an insight into brief cognitive behaviour therapy. Although the approach we described was largely based on the work of Aaron Beck, we also included ideas and techniques developed by Albert Ellis and Arnold Lazarus as brief therapy takes a pragmatic stance and incorporates clinically useful strategies. This reflects the integrative nature of cognitive behaviour therapy.

We never cease to be amazed by the number of therapists we meet who claim to be practising one of the cognitive behavioural therapies. Yet, on further discussion we discover that they have never attended an extended training programme that focuses specifically on the approach. The situation is compounded when we discover that their clinical supervisor has not been trained in the approach either. Of course, this raises a number of ethical and professional issues related to competency. This book may make the approach seem deceptively simple. However, in our experience it may take some years for a therapist to grasp the theory and have the requisite cognitive behaviour therapy skills necessary to be proficient in its practice. Initially, we would recommend that therapists interested in this approach attend a number of relevant workshops or conferences to discover whether cognitive behaviour therapy is suited to their personality and general view of life. If they are still keen to learn more about the approach and want to practise it, then it is important to attend an extended training programme and receive appropriate supervision.

Specific training in cognitive behaviour therapy is available at the Centre for Cognitive Behaviour Therapy in London. The Centre is run in association with the Centre for Stress Management and the services include short two-day courses and an advanced modular training programme. There are a number of training centres or universities offering cognitive, cognitive behaviour and/or rational emotive behaviour therapy training in Britain and the USA. We recommend that readers interested in training or relevant continuing professional development contact the various professional cognitive behaviour therapy associations and seek their advice regarding courses or accreditation. The British Association for Behaviour and

Cognitive Psychotherapies accredits therapists and runs conferences and workshops. We provide below contact details:

Centre for Cognitive Behaviour Therapy and Centre for Stress Management
156 Westcombe Hill
Blackheath
London SE3 7DH
Tel: +44 (0) 20 8853 1122
Fax: +44 (0) 20 8293 1441
Website: http://www.managingstress.com
email: admin@managingstress.com

British Association for Behaviour and Cognitive Psychotherapies
PO Box 9
Accrington BB5 2GD
Tel: +44 (0) 125 487 5277
Website: http://www.babcp.org.uk
email: membership@babcp.org.uk

International Association for Cognitive Psychotherapy
Membership Office
Department of Psychology
University of South Mississippi
Hattiesburg
MS 39406
USA
Fax: 001 601 266 5580
Website: http://iacp.asu.edu

The authors would be interested to hear your views about this book. Please write to us at the Centre for Cognitive Behaviour Therapy (address above).

References

Abramson, L.Y., Seligman, M.E.P. and Teasdale, J.D. (1978) 'Learned helplessness in humans: critique and reformulation', *Journal of Abnormal Psychology*, 87: 49–74.

Agras, W.S., Rossiter, E.M., Arnow, B., Schneider, J.A., Telch, C.F., Raeburn, S.D., Bruce, B., Perl, M. and Koran, L.M. (1992) 'Pharmacological and cognitive-behavioral treatment for bulimia nervosa: a controlled comparison', *American Journal of Psychiatry*, 149: 82–7.

Alexander, F. and French, T.M. (1974) *Psychoanalytic Therapy: Principles and Application*. Lincoln: University of Nebraska Press (original work published 1946).

American Psychiatric Association (1994) *Diagnostic and Statistical Manual of Mental Disorders*, 4th edn. Washington, DC: APA.

Andrews, G., Crino, R., Hunt, C., Lampe, L. and Page, A. (1992) *A List of Essential Psychotherapies. Proceedings of the Annual Conference of the Royal Australian and New Zealand College of Psychiatrists*. Canberra: Royal Australian and New Zealand College of Psychiatrists.

Andrews, G., Crino, R., Hunt, C., Lampe, L. and Page, A. (1994) *The Treatment of Anxiety Disorders: Clinician's Guide and Patient Manuals*. Cambridge: Cambridge University Press.

Arnold, M. (1960) *Emotions and Personality*, vol. 1. New York: Columbia University Press.

Bard, J.A. (1973) 'Rational proselytizing', *Rational Living*, 12 (1): 2–6.

Bard, J.A. (1980) *Rational-Emotional Therapy in Practice*. Champaign, IL: Research Press.

Barkham, M. and Shapiro, D. (1988) 'Psychotherapy in two sessions: a research protocol'. Social and Applied Psychology Unit Memo no. 891, University of Sheffield, Department of Psychology.

Barkham, M., Moorey, E.J. and Davis, G. (1992) 'Cognitive-behavioural therapy in two-plus-one sessions: a pilot field trial', *Behavioural Psychotherapy*, 20: 147–54.

Barlow, D.H. (1988) *Anxiety and its Disorders: The Nature and Treatment of Anxiety and Panic*. New York: Guilford Press.

Barlow, D.H. and Craske, M.G. (1989) *Mastery of Your Anxiety and Panic*. Albany, NY: Graywind Publications.

Barlow, D.H., Craske, M.G., Cerney, J.A. and Klosko, J.S. (1989) 'Behavioral treatment of panic disorder', *Behavior Therapy*, 20: 261–8.

Bartlett, F.C. (1932) *Remembering*. Cambridge: Cambridge University Press.

Baucom, D., Sayers, S. and Scher, T. (1990) 'Supplementary behavior marital therapy with cognitive restructuring and emotional expressiveness training: an outcome investigation', *Journal of Consulting and Clinical Psychology*, 58: 636–45.

Beck, A.T. (1963) 'Thinking and depression: I. Idiosyncratic content and cognitive distortions', *Archives of General Psychiatry*, 9: 324–33.

Beck, A.T. (1964) 'Thinking and depression: II. Theory and therapy', *Archives of General Psychiatry*, 10: 561–71.

Beck, A.T. (1967) *Depression: Clinical, Experimental and Theoretical Aspects.* New York: Harper and Row.

Beck, A.T. (1970) 'Role of fantasies in psychotherapy and psychopathology', *Journal of Nervous Mental Disorders*, 150: 3–17.

Beck, A.T. (1975) *Depression: Causes and Treatment.* Philadelphia: University of Pennsylvania Press.

Beck, A.T. (1976) *Cognitive Therapy and the Emotional Disorders.* Harmondsworth: Penguin.

Beck, A.T. (1978) *Depression Inventory.* Philadelphia: Center for Cognitive Therapy.

Beck, A.T. (1987) 'Cognitive approaches to panic disorder: theory and therapy', in S. Rachman and J. Maser (eds), *Panic: Psychological Perspectives.* Hillsdale, NJ: Erlbaum.

Beck, A.T., Ward, C.H., Mendelson, M., Mock, J.E. and Erbaugh, J.K. (1961) 'An inventory for measuring depression', *Archives of General Psychiatry*, 4: 561–71.

Beck, A.T., Kovacs, M. and Weissman, A. (1971) 'Assessment of suicidal ideation: the scale for suicidal ideation', *Journal of Consultancy and Clinical Psychology*, 47: 343–52.

Beck, A.T. and Greenberg, R.L. (1974) *Coping with Depression.* New York: Institute for Rational Living.

Beck, A.T. and Steer, R.A. (1987) *Manual for the Revised Beck Depression Inventory.* San Antonio, TX: Psychological Corporation.

Beck, A.T. and Steer, R.A. (1990) *Manual for the Beck Anxiety Inventory.* New York: Psychological Corporation.

Beck, A.T., Schuyler, D. and Herman, I. (1974a) 'Development of suicidal intent scales', in A.T. Beck, H.L.P. Resnick and D.J. Lettie (eds), *The Prediction of Suicide.* Maryland: Charles Press.

Beck, A.T., Weissman, A., Lester, D. and Trexter, L. (1974b) 'The measurement of pessimism: the hopelessness scale', *Journal of Consulting and Clinical Psychology*, 42: 861–5.

Beck, A.T., Weissman, A. and Kovacs, M. (1976). 'Alcoholism, hopelessness and suicidal behaviour', *Journal of Studies on Alcohol*, 37: 66–77.

Beck, A.T., Rush, A.J., Shaw, B.F. and Emery, G. (1979) *Cognitive Therapy of Depression.* New York: Guilford Press.

Beck, A.T., Emery, G. and Greenberg, R.L. (1985) *Anxiety Disorders and Phobias.* New York, NY: Basic Books.

Beck, A.T., Freeman, A., Pretzer, J., Davis, D.D., Fleming, B., Ottavani, R., Beck, J., Simon, K.M., Padesky, K., Meyer, J. and Trexier, L. (1990a) *Cognitive Therapy of Personality Disorders.* New York: Guilford Press.

Beck, A.T., Steer, R.A., Epstein, N. and Brown, G. (1990b) 'The Beck self-concept test', *Psychological Assessment. A Journal of Consulting and Clinical Psychology*, 2: 191–7.

Beck, J.S. (1995) *Cognitive Therapy: Basics and Beyond.* New York: Guilford Press.

Benson, H. (1976) *The Relaxation Response.* London: Collins.

Bernstein, D.A. and Borkovec, T.D. (1973) *Progressive Relaxation Training: A Manual for the Helping Professions.* Champaign, IL: Research Press.

Blackburn, I.M. and Eunson, K.M. (1988) 'A content analysis of thoughts and emotions elicited from depressed patients during cognitive therapy', *British Journal of Medical Psychology*, 62: 23–33.

Block, B.M. and Lefkovitz, P.M. (1991) 'American association for partial hospitalization: standards and guidelines for partial hospitalization', *International Journal of Partial Hospitalization*, 7 (1): 3–11.

Bonarius, J.C.J. (1970) 'Fixed role therapy – a double paradox', *British Journal of Medical Psychology*, 43: 213–19.

Bowers, W.A. (1990) 'Treatment of depressed inpatients: cognitive therapy plus medication, relaxation plus medication, and medication alone', *British Journal of Psychiatry*, 156: 73–8.

Brewin, C.R. and Bradley, C. (1989) 'Patient preferences and randomised clinical trials', *British Medical Journal*, 299: 313–15.

British Psychological Society (1990) *Psychotherapy Services in the NHS: The Need for Organisational Change*. Leicester: BPS.

Budman, S.H. (1981) 'Avoiding dropouts in couples therapy', in A.S. Gurman (ed.), *Questions and Answers in the Practice of Family Therapy*. New York: Brunner/ Mazel. pp. 71–3.

Budman, S.H. and Clifford, M. (1979) 'Short-term group therapy for couples in a health maintenance organisation', *Professional Psychology: Reseach and Practice*, 10: 419–29.

Budman S.H. and Gurman, A.S. (1988) *Theory and Practice of Brief Therapy*. London: Guilford Press.

Budman, S.H., Clifford, M., Bader, L. and Bader, B. (1981) 'Experiential pre-group preparation and screening', *Group*, 5 (1): 19–26.

Burns, D.D. (1980) *Feeling Good: The New Mood Therapy*. New York: Signet.

Burns, D.D. (1989) *The Feeling Good Handbook*. New York: Penguin.

Butcher, J.N. and Koss, M.P. (1978) 'Research on brief and crisis oriented therapies', in S. Garfield and A.E. Bergin (eds), *Handbook of Psychotherapy and Behavior Change*, 2nd edn. New York: Wiley, pp. 725–68.

Butler, G. and Booth, R.G. (1991) 'Developing psychological treatments for generalized anxiety disorder', in R.M. Rapee and D.H. Barlow (eds), *Chronic Anxiety. Generalized Anxiety Disorder and Mixed Anxiety-Depression*. New York: Guilford Press, pp. 187–209.

Butler, G., Fennell, M., Robson, D. and Gelder, M. (1991) 'Comparison of behavior therapy and cognitive-behavior therapy in the treatment of generalized anxiety disorder', *Journal of Consulting and Clinical Psychology*, 59: 167–75.

Callahan, R. (1985) *Five Minute Phobia Cure*. Wilmington, DE: Enterprise.

Carrington, P. (1993) 'Modern forms of meditation', in P.M. Lehrer and R.L. Woolfolk (eds), *Principles and Practice of Stress Management*, 2nd edn. New York: Guilford Press.

Cautela, J. (1967) 'Covert sensitization', *Psychological Reports*, 20: 459–68.

Cautela, J. (1971) 'Covert conditioning', in A. Jacobs and L. Sachs (eds), *The Psychology of Private Events: Perspectives on Covert Response Systems*. New York: Academic Press.

Clark, D.M. (1986) 'A cognitive approach to panic', *Behaviour Research and Therapy*, 24: 461–70.

Clark, D.M. (1988) 'A cognitive model of panic attacks', in S. Rachman and J.D. Maser (eds), *Panic, Psychological Perspectives*. Hillsdale, NJ: Erlbaum, pp. 71–90.

Clark, D.M. (1989) 'Anxiety states: panic and generalised anxiety', in K. Hawton, P. Salkovskis, J. Kirk and D. Clark (eds), *Cognitive Behaviour Therapy for Psychiatric Problems: A Practical Guide*. Oxford: Oxford University Press.

Corcoran, K. and Fischer, J. (1987) *Measures in Clinical Practice*. New York: Free Press.

Craig, G. (1997) *Six days at the VA: Using Emotional Freedom Therapy*, videotape. Available from Gary Craig, 1102 Redwood Blvd, Novato, CA 94947, USA.

Cummings, N.A. (1990) 'Brief intermittent psychotherapy throughout the life cycle', in J.K. Zeig and S.G. Gilligan (eds), *Brief Therapy: Myths, Methods and Metaphors*. New York: Brunner/Mazel.

Cummings, N.A. and Sayama, M. (1995) *Focussed Psychotherapy: A Casebook of Brief, Intermittent Psychotherapy Throughout the Life Cycle*. New York: Brunner/Mazel.

Curwen, B. (1997) 'Medical and psychiatric assessment', in S. Palmer and G. McMahon (eds), *Client Assessment*. London: Sage.

Dinnage, R. (1988) *One to One: Experiences of Psychotherapy*. London: Viking.

Dobson, K.S. (1989) 'A meta-analysis of the efficacy of cognitive therapy for depression', *Journal of Consulting and Clinical Psychology*, 57: 414–19.

Dryden, W. (1991) *Reason and Therapeutic Change*. London: Whurr.

Dryden, W. (1995) *Brief Rational Emotive Behaviour Therapy*. Chichester: Wiley.

Dryden, W. and Feltham, C. (1992) *Brief Counselling*. Buckingham: Open University Press.

Dryden, W. and Gordon, J. (1990) *Think Your Way To Happiness*. London: Sheldon.

Dryden, W. and Gordon, J. (1992) *Think Rationally: A Brief Guide To Overcoming Your Emotional Problems*. London: Centre For Rational Emotive Behaviour Therapy.

Durham, R.C. and Allan, T. (1993) 'Psychological treatment of generalised anxiety disorder. A review of the clinical significance of results in outcome studies since 1980', *British Journal of Psychiatry*, 163: 19–26.

Edgell, B. (1926) *Mental Life: An Introduction to Psychology*. London: Methuen.

Ellis, A. (1962) *Reason and Emotion in Psychotherapy*. New York: Lyle Stuart.

Ellis, A. (1977) 'The basic clinical theory of rational-emotive therapy', in A. Ellis and R. Grieger (eds), *Handbook of Rational-Emotive Therapy*. New York: Springer.

Ellis, A. (1977a) 'Fun as psychotherapy', *Rational Living*, 12 (1): 2–6.

Ellis, A. (1977b) *A Garland Of Rational Humorous Songs*, cassette recording and songbook. New York: Institute For Rational-Emotive Therapy.

Ellis, A. (1979) 'The practice of rational-emotive therapy', in A. Ellis and J.M. Whitely (eds), *Theoretical and Empirical Foundations of Rational-Emotive Therapy*. Monterey, CA: Brooks/Cole.

Ellis, A. (1982) 'Intimacy in rational-emotive therapy', in M. Fisher and G. Stricker (eds), *Intimacy*. New York: Plenum.

Ellis, A. (1985) *Overcoming Resistance: Rational-Emotive Therapy with Difficult Clients*. New York: Springer.

Ellis, A. (1986) 'Anxiety about anxiety: the use of hypnosis with rational-emotive therapy', in E.T. Dowd and J.M. Healy (eds), *Case Studies in Hypnotherapy*. New York: Guilford Press, pp. 3–11.

Ellis, A. (1988) *How to Stubbornly Refuse to Make Yourself Miserable About Anything – Yes Anything!* Secaucus, NJ: Lyle Stuart.

Ellis, A. (1993) 'Rational-emotive imagery and hypnosis', in J.W. Rhue, S.J. Lynn and I. Kirsch (eds), *Handbook of Clinical Hypnosis*. Washington, DC: American Psychological Association, pp. 173–86.

Ellis, A. (1994) *Reason and Emotion in Psychotherapy*, 2nd edn. New York: Birch Lane Press.

Ellis, A. (1995) *Better, Deeper, and Enduring Brief Psychotherapy: The Rational Emotive Behaviour Therapy Approach*. New York: Brunner/Mazel.

Ellis, A. and Harper, R.A. (1997) *A Guide To Rational Living*. North Hollywood, CA: Wilshire.

Ellis, A., Gordon, J., Neenan, M. and Palmer, S. (1998) *Stress Counseling: A Rational Emotive Behavior Approach*. New York: Springer Publishing.

Emmelkamp, P.M.G. (1994) 'Behavior therapy with adults', in A.E. Bergin and S.L. Garfield (eds), *Handbook of Psychotherapy and Behavior Change*, 4th edn. New York: Wiley.

Emmelkamp, P.M.G., Kuipers, A.C. M. and Eggeraat, J.B. (1978) 'Cognitive modification versus prolonged exposure in vivo: a comparison with agoraphobics as subjects', *Behaviour Research and Therapy*, 16: 33–41.

Epting, F. (1984) *Personal Construct Counselling and Psychotherapy*. New York. Wiley.

Fagan, M. and Shepherd, I. (1970) *Gestalt Therapy Now*. Palo Alto, CA: Science and Behavior Books.

Fairburn, C.G. and Cooper, P.J. (1989) 'Eating disorders', in D.M.Garner and P.E. Garfinkel (eds), *Handbook of Psychotherapy for Anorexia Nervosa and Bulimia*. New York: Guilford Press.

Fairburn, C.G., Jones, R., Peveler, R.C., Hope, R.A. and Doll, H.A. (1991) 'Three psychological treatments for bulimia nervosa: a comparative trial', *Archives of General Psychiatry*, 48: 463–9.

Feder, B. and Ronall, R. (eds) (1980) *Beyond the Hot Seat: Gestalt Approaches to Group*. New York. Brunner/Mazel.

Feltham, C. (1997) *Time-Limited Counselling*. London: Sage.

Fennell, M.J.V. (1989) 'Depression', in K. Hawton, P. Salkovskis, J. Kirk and D. Clark (eds), *Cognitive Behaviour Therapy for Psychiatric Problems: A Practical Guide*. Oxford: Oxford University Press.

Fennell, M.J.V. and Teasdale, J.D. (1987) 'Cognitive therapy for depression: individual differences and the process of change', *Cognitive Therapy and Research*, 11: 253–71.

Figley, C. (1997) 'The active ingredients of the power therapies'. Keynote presentation at the Power Therapies: A Conference for the Integrative and Innovative Use of EMDR, TFT, EFT, Advanced NLP, and TIR. Lakewood: Colorado.

Foa, E.B. (1979) 'Failure in treating obsessive compulsives', *Behaviour Research and Therapy*, 17: 169–79.

Foa, E.B. and Kozak, M.J. (1986) 'Emotional processing of fear: exposure to corrective information', *Psychological Bulletin*, 99: 20–35.

Foa, E.B., Grayson, J.B. Steketee, G., Doppelt, H.G., Turner, R.M. and Latimer, P.R. (1983a) 'Success and failure in behavioral treatment of obsessive compulsives', *Journal of Consulting and Clinical Psychology*, 51: 287–97.

Foa, E.B., Steketee, G., Grayson, J.B. and Doppelt, H.G. (1983b) 'Treatment of obsessive-compulsives: when do we fail?, in E.B. Foa and P.M.G. Emmelkamp (eds), *Failures in Behavior Therapy*. New York: Wiley.

Foa, E.B., Steketee, G. and Ozarow, B.J. (1985) 'Behaviour therapy with obsessive compulsives: from therapy to treatment', in M. Mavissakalian, S.M. Turner and L. Michelsen (eds), *Obsessive Compulsive Disorder: Psychological and Pharmacological Treatments*. New York: Plenum Press.

Foa, E.B., Steketee, G. and Olasov Rothbaum, B. (1989) 'Behavioral/cognitive conceptualization of post-traumatic stress disorder', *Behavior Therapy*, 20: 155–76.

Frances, A.J. and Clarkin, J.F. (1981) 'No treatment as the prescription of choice', *Archives of General Psychiatry*, 38: 542–5.

Freeman, A. and Jackson, J.T. (1998) 'Cognitive behavioural treatment of personality disorders', in N. Tarrier, A. Wells and G. Haddock (eds), *Treating Complex Cases*. Chichester: Wiley.

Gafner, G. and Young, C. (1998) 'Hypnosis as an adjuvant treatment in chronic paranoid schizophrenia', *Contemporary Hypnosis*, 15 (4): 223–6.

Garfield, S.L. (1971) 'Research on client variable in psychotherapy', in A.E. Bergin and S. Garfield (eds), *Handbook of Psychotherapy and Behavior Change*. New York: Wiley, pp. 271–98.

Garfield, S.L. (1978) 'Research on client variable in psychotherapy', in S.L. Garfield and A.E. Bergin (eds), *Handbook of Psychotherapy and Behavior Change*, 2nd edn. New York: Wiley, pp. 191–232.

Garfield, S.L. (1986) 'Research on client variable in psychotherapy', in S.L. Garfield and A.E. Bergin (eds), *Handbook of Psychotherapy and Behavior Change*, 3rd edn. New York: Wiley.

Garfield, S.L. (1995) *Psychotherapy: An Eclectic-Integrative Approach*, 2nd edn. New York: Wiley.

Garner, D.M., Rockert, W., Davis, R., Garner, M.V., Olmstead, M.P. and Eagle, M. (1993) 'Comparison of cognitive-behavioral and supportive-expressive therapy for bulimia nervosa', *American Journal of Psychiatry*, 150: 37–46.

Gerbode, F. (1988) *Beyond Psychology. An Introduction to Metapsychology*. Palo Alto, CA: IRM Press.

Gilligan, C. (1982) *In a Different Voice*. Cambridge, MA: Harvard University Press.

Goffman, E. (1963) *Stigma: Notes on the Management of Spoiled Identity*. Harmondsworth: Penguin.

Goldfried, M. (1971) 'Systematic desensitization as training in self-control', *Journal of Consulting and Clinical Psychology*, 37: 228–34.

Goldfried, M.R. and Davison, G.C. (1976) *Clinical Behavior Therapy*. New York: Holt Rinehart and Winston.

Grant, S., Margison, F. and Powell, A. (1991) 'The future of psychotherapy services', *Psychiatric Bulletin*, 15: 174–9.

Greenberger, D. and Padesky, C.A. (1995) *Mind Over Mood. A Cognitive Therapy Treatment Manual for Clients*. New York: Guilford Press.

Hackmann, A. (1998) 'Cognitive therapy panic and agoraphobia: working with complex cases', in N. Turner, A. Wells and G. Haddock (eds) *Treating Complex Cases: The Cognitive Behavioural Therapy Approach*. Chichester: John Wiley & Sons.

Hamilton, M. (1959) 'The assessment of anxiety states by rating', *British Journal of Medical Psychology*, 32: 50–5.

Hamilton, M. (1960) 'A rating scale for depression', *Journal of Neurological and Neurosurgical Psychiatry*, 23: 56–62.

Hartland, J. (1971) *Medical and Dental Hypnosis and its Clinical Applications*. London: Baillière Tindall.

Hawton, K. and Kirk, J. (1989) 'Problem-solving', in K. Hawton, P. Salkovskis, J. Kirk and D. Clark (eds), *Cognitive Behaviour Therapy for Psychiatric Problems: A Practical Guide*. Oxford: Oxford University Press.

Hollon, S.D. and Kris, M.R. (1984) 'Cognitive factors in clinical research and practice', *Clinical Psychology Review*, 4: 35–76.

Howard, K.I., Kopta, S.M., Krause, M.S. and Orlinsky, D.E. (1986) 'The dose–effect relationship in psychotherapy', *American Psychologist*, 41: 159–64.

Howard, K.I., Davidson, V.V., O'Mahoney, M.T., Orlinsky, D.E. and Brown, K.P. (1989) 'Patterns of psychotherapy utilisation', *American Journal of Psychiatry*, 146: 775–8.

Hoyt, M.F. (1989) 'On time in brief therapy', in R. Wells and V. Gianetti (eds), *Handbook of the Brief Psychotherapies*. New York: Plenum Press.

Hunt, C. and Singh, M. (1991) 'Generalized anxiety disorder', *International Review of Psychiatry*, 3: 215–29.

Jacobson, E.J. (1938) *Progressive Relaxation*. Chicago: University of Chicago Press.

James, I. and Palmer, S. (1996) 'Professional therapeutic titles: myths and realities'. Division of Counselling Psychology Occasional Papers, vol. 2. British Psychological Society.

Karst, T.O. and Trexler, L.D. (1970) 'Initial study using fixed-role and rational-emotive therapy in treating public-speaking anxiety', *Journal Consulting Clinical Psychology*, 34: 360–6.

Kelly, G.A. (1955) *The Psychology of Personal Constructs*, vols 1 and 2. New York: Norton.

Kirk, J. (1989) 'Cognitive-behavioural assessment', in K. Hawton, P.M. Salkovskis, J. Kirk and D.M. Clark (eds), *Cognitive Behaviour Therapy for Psychiatric Problems*. Oxford: Oxford University Press.

Kirsch, I., Montgomery, G. and Sapirstein, G. (1995) 'Hypnosis as an adjunct to cognitive-behavioural psychotherapy: a meta-analysis', *Journal of Consulting and Clinical Psychology*, 63: 214–20.

Kirsch, I., Capafons, A., Cardeña-Buelna, E. and Amigó, S. (1999) *Clinical Hypnosis and Self-Regulation: Cognitive-Behavioral Perspectives*. Washington, DC: American Psychological Association.

Korzybski, A. (1933) *Science and Sanity*. San Francisco: International Society of General Semantics.

Lazarus, A.A. (1971) *Behavior Therapy and Beyond*. New York: McGraw-Hill.

Lazarus, A.A. (1973) 'Hypnosis as a facilitator in behavior therapy', *International Journal of Clinical and Experimental Hypnosis*, 21: 25–31.

Lazarus, A.A. (1977) 'Toward an egoless state of being', in A. Ellis and R. Grieger (eds), *Handbook of Rational-Emotive Therapy*. New York: McGraw-Hill.

Lazarus, A.A. (1981) *The Practice of Multimodal Therapy: Systematic, Comprehensive and Effective Psychotherapy*. New York: McGraw-Hill.

Lazarus, A.A. (1984) *In The Mind's Eye*. New York: Guilford Press.

Lazarus, A.A. (1989) *The Practice of Multimodal Therapy: Systemic, Comprehensive and Effective Psychotherapy*. Baltimore, MA: Johns Hopkins University Press.

Lazarus, A.A. (1997) *Brief but Comprehensive Psychotherapy: the Multimodal Way*. New York: Springer.

Lazarus, A.A. (1999) 'A multimodal framework for clinical hypnosis', in I. Kirsch, A. Capafons, E. Cardeña-Buelna and S. Amigó (eds), *Clinical Hypnosis and Self-Regulation: Cognitive-Behavioral Perspectives*. Washington, DC: American Psychological Association.

Lazarus, A.A. and Fay, A. (1990) 'Brief psychotherapy: tautology or oxymoron', in J.K. Zeig and S. Gilligan (eds), *Brief Therapy: Myths, Methods, and Metaphors*. New York: Brunner/Mazel.

Lazarus, A.A., Kanner, A. and Folkman, S. (1980) 'Emotions: a cognitive phenomenological analysis', in R. Plutchik and H. Kellerman (eds), *Theory of Emotions*. New York: Academic Press.

Lazarus, A.A., Lazarus, C. and Fay, A. (1993) *Don't Believe It For A Minute: Forty Toxic Ideas That Are Driving You Crazy*. San Luis Obispo, CA: Impact Publishers.

Lazarus, R. (1966) *Psychotherapy and Patient Relationships*. New York: McGraw-Hill.

Levin, S. (1962) 'Indications for analysis and problems of analyzability: discussion', *Psychoanalytic Quarterly*, 33: 528–31.

Lewinsohn, P.M., Sullivan, M.J. and Grosscup, S.J. (1982) 'Behavioral therapy: clinical applications', in A.J. Rush (ed.), *Short-term Psychotherapies for Depression*. New York: Wiley, pp. 50–87.

Ley, P. (1979) 'Memory for medical information', *British Journal of Social and Clinical Psychology*, 18: 245–55.

Liebowitz, M.R., Gorman, J., Fyer, A.J. and Klein, D.F. (1985) 'Social phobia: review of a neglected anxiety disorder', *Archives of General Psychiatry*, 42: 729–36.

Linehan, M.M. (1985) 'The reason for living scale', in P.A. Keller and L.G. Ritts (eds), *Innovations in Clinical Practice: A Source Book*, vol. 4. Sarasota, FL: Professional Resource Exchange.

Lonner, W.J. and Sondberg, N.D. (1995) 'Assessment in cross-cultural counseling and therapy', in P. Pederson (ed.), *Handbook of Cross-Cultural Counseling and Therapy*. Westport, CT: Greenwood Press.

Los Angeles Center for Suicide Prevention (1973) *Los Angeles Suicide Prevention Scale*. Los Angeles: LSCSP.

Lucock, M.P. and Salkovskis, P.M. (1988) 'Cognitive factors in social anxiety and its treatment', *Behaviour Research and Therapy*, 26: 297–302.

Lukas, S. (1993) *Where to Start and What to Ask: An Assessment Handbook*. London: W.W. Norton.

MacCarthy, B. (1998) 'Clinical work with ethnic minorities', in F. Watts (ed.), *New Developments in Clinical Psychology*, vol. 2. Chichester: Wiley.

Macaskill, N.D. and Macaskill, A. (1991) 'Cognitive therapy for depression: the efficacy of minimal intervention programmes', *Bulletin of the Association of Behavioural Clinicians*, 10: 13–20.

McGuigan, F.J. (1993) 'Progressive relaxation: origins, principles, and clinical applications', in P.M. Lehrer and R.L. Woolfolk (eds), *Principles and Practice of Stress Management*, 2nd edn. New York: Guilford Press.

McMahon, G. (1997) 'Client history taking and associated administration', in S. Palmer and G. McMahon (eds), *Client Assessment*. London: Sage.

McMullin, R.E. (1986) *Handbook of Cognitive Therapy Techniques*. New York: Norton.

Mahoney, M. and Thoresen, C. (1974) *Self-Control: Power to the Person*. Monterey, CA: Brooks/Cole.

Malan, D.H. (1979) *Individual Psychotherapy and the Science of Psychodynamics*. Cambridge: Butterworths.

Marks, I.M. (1986) *Living with Fear*. New York: McGraw-Hill.

Marks, I.M. (1989) 'Agoraphobia and panic disorder', in R. Baker (ed.), *Panic Disorder: Theory, Research and Practice*. Chichester: Wiley.

Mattick, R.P. and Peters, L. (1988) 'Treatment of severe social phobia: effects of guided exposure with and without cognitive restructuring', *Journal of Consulting and Clinical Psychology*, 56: 251–60.

Mattick, R.P., Peters, L. and Clarke, J.C. (1989) 'Exposure and cognitive restructuring for social phobia: a controlled study', *Behavior Therapy*, 20: 3–23.

Maultsby, M.C. (1968) 'The pamphlet as a therapeutic aid', *Rational Living*, 3: 31–5.

Maultsby, M.C., Jr. (1975) *Rational Behavior Therapy*. Englewood Cliffs, NJ: Prentice Hall.

Maultsby, M.C., Jr and Ellis, A. (1974) *Techniques For Using Rational-Emotive Imagery*. New York: Institute For Rational-Emotive Therapy.

Meichenbaum, D. (1975) 'A self-instructional approach to stress management: a proposal for stress inoculation training', in I. Sarason and C. Spielberger (eds), *Stress and Anxiety*, vol. 2. New York: Wiley.

Meichenbaum, D. (1977) *Cognitive-Behavior Modification: An Integrative Approach*. New York: Plenum Press.

Meichenbaum, D. (1985) *Stress Inoculation Training*. New York: Pergamon.

Miller, I.W., Norman, W.H., Keitner, G.I., Bishop, S.B. and Dow, M.G. (1989) 'Cognitive-behavioral treatment of depressed inpatients', *Behavior Therapy*, 20: 25–47.

Milne, D. (1987) *Evaluating Mental Health Practice: Methods and Application*. London: Croom Helm.

Milner, P. and Palmer, S. (1998) *Integrative Stress Counselling: An Humanistic, Problem-Focused Approach*. London: Cassell.

Moore, R.H. (1993) 'Traumatic incident reduction: a cognitive-emotive treatment of post-traumatic stress disorder', in W. Dryden and L.K. Hill (eds), *Innovations in Rational-Emotive Therapy*. Newbury Park: Sage.

Morrison, J. (1995) *The First Interview*. New York: Guilford Press.

Neenan, M. and Palmer, S. (1998) 'A cognitive-behavioural approach to tackling stress', *Counselling*, 9 (4): 315–19.

Newman, F.L. and Howard, K.I. (1986) 'Therapeutic effort, treatment outcome and national health policy', *American Psychologist*, 41: 181–7.

Neugarten, B.L. (1979) 'Time, age and the life cycle', *American Journal of Psychiatry*, 136: 149–55.

Niemeyer, R.A. and Feixas, G. (1990) 'The role of homework and skill acquisition in the outcome of group cognitive therapy for depression', *Behavior Therapy*, 21 (3): 281–92.

Nisbett, R.E. and Ross, L. (1980) *Human Inference: Strategies and Shortcomings of Social Judgement*. Englewood Cliffs, NJ. Prentice Hall.

Ochberg, F.M. (1996) 'The counting method for ameliorating traumatic memories', *Journal of Traumatic Stress*, 9: 866–73.

Orinsky, D.E. and Howard, R.I. (1986) 'The relation of process to outcome in psychotherapy', in S.L. Garfield and A.E. Bergin (eds), *Handbook of Psychotherapy and Behavior Change*, 3rd edn. New York: Wiley.

Ost, L.G. (1987) 'Applied relaxation: description of a coping technique and review of controlled studies', *Behaviour Research and Therapy*, 26: 13–22.

Ost, L.G., Jerremalm, A. and Johansson, J. (1981) 'Individual response patterns and the effects of different behavioral methods in the treatment of social phobia', *Behavior Research and Therapy*, 19: 1–16.

Padesky, C.A. (1994) 'Schema change processes in cognitive therapy', *Clinical Psychology and Psychotherapy*, 1 (5): 267–78.

Padesky, C.A. and Greenberger, D. (1995) *Clinician's Guide to Mind Over Mood*. New York: Guilford Press.

Palmer, S. (1992) 'Guidelines and contra-indications for teaching relaxation as a stress management technique', *Journal of The Institute of Health Education*, 30 (1): 25–30.

Palmer, S. (1993a) 'The "deserted island technique": a method of demonstrating how preferential and musturbatory beliefs can lead to different emotions', *Rational Emotive Behaviour Therapist*, 1 (1): 12–14.

Palmer, S. (1993b) *Multimodal Techniques: Relaxation and Hypnosis*. London: Centre for Stress Management and Centre for Multimodal Therapy.

Palmer, S. (1994) 'Stress management and counselling: a problem-solving approach', *Stress News*, 5 (3): 2–3.

Palmer, S. (1997a) 'Self-acceptance: concept, techniques and interventions', *Rational Emotive Behaviour Therapist*, 5 (1): 4–30.

Palmer, S. (1997b) 'A rational emotive behaviour approach to hypnosis', *Rational Emotive Behaviour Therapist*, 5 (1): 34–54.

Palmer, S. (1999) 'Effective counselling across cultures', in S. Palmer and P. Laungani (eds), *Counselling Across Cultures*. London: Sage.

Palmer, S. and Burton, T. (1996) *Dealing With People Problems At Work*. Maidenhead: McGraw-Hill.

Palmer, S. and Dryden, W. (1995) *Counselling For Stress Problems*. London: Sage.

Palmer, S. and McMahon, G. (eds) (1997) *Client Assessment*. London: Sage.

Palmer, S. and Neenan, M. (1998) 'Double imagery procedure', *Rational Emotive Behaviour Therapist*, 6 (2): 89–92.

Palmer, S. and Strickland, L. (1996) *Stress Management: A Quick Guide*. Dunstable: Folens.

Parker, I., Georgaca, E., Harper, D., McLaughlin, T. and Stowell-Smith, M. (1995) *Deconstructing Psychopathology*. London: Sage.

Parloff, M.B., Waskow, I.E. and Wolfe, B.E. (1978) 'Research on therapist variables in relation to process and outcome', in S.L. Garfield and A.E. Bergin (eds), *Handbook of Psychotherapy and Behavior Change*, 2nd edn. New York: Wiley, pp. 233–82.

Parry, G. (1992) 'Improving psychotherapy services: applications of research, audit and evaluation', *British Journal of Clinical Psychology*, 31: 3–19.

Parry, G. and Watts, F.N. (1989) *Behavioural and Mental Health Research: A Handbook of Skills and Methods*. Hove and London: Erlbaum.

Penava S.J., Otto, M.W. and Pollack, M.H. (1995) 'An effect size analysis of treatment outcome studies for post-traumatic stress disorder'. Paper presented at the World Congress of Behavioural and Cognitive Therapies, July, Copenhagen.

Perls, F. (1969a) *Gestalt Therapy Verbatim*. Lafayette, CA: Real People Press.

Perls, F. (1969b) *In and Out of the Garbage Pail*. Lafayette, CA: Real People Press.

Perls, F. (1973) *The Gestalt Approach*. Palo Alto, CA: Science and Behavior Books.

Persons, J.B. (1989) *Cognitive Therapy in Practice. A Case Formulation Approach*. New York: Norton.

Persons, J.B., Burns, D.D. and Perloff, J.M. (1988) 'Predictors of dropout and outcome in cognitive therapy for depression in a private practice setting', *Cognitive Therapy and Research*, 12: 557–75.

Pfister, O. (1917) *The Psychoanalytic Method*. London: Kogan Page.

Piaget, J. (1954) *The Construction of Reality in the Child*. New York: Basic Books.

Polster, E. and Polster, M. (1973) *Gestalt Therapy Integrated: Contours of Theory and Practice*. New York: Brunner/Mazel.

Pretzer, J.L. (1983) 'Borderline personality disorder: too complex for cognitive-behavioural approaches?' Paper presented at meeting of the American Psychological Association, Anaheim, CA. (ERIC document reproduction service no. ED 243007).

Rack, P. (1982) *Race, Culture and Mental Disorder*. London: Routledge.

Rehm, L.P. (1982) 'Self-management in depression', in P. Karoly and F.H. Kanfer (eds), *Self-management and Behavior Change: From Theory to Practice*. New York: Pergamon, pp. 552–70.

Ridley, C.R. (1995) *Overcoming Unintentional Racism in Counseling and Therapy: A Practitioner's Guide to Intentional Intervention*. Thousand Oaks, CA: Sage.

Robins, E., Gassner. S., Kayes. J., Wilkinson, R.H. and Murphy, G.E. (1959) 'The communication of suicidal intent: a study of 134 successful (completed) suicides', *American Journal of Psychiatry*, 115: 724–33.

Rosen, H. (1988) 'The constructivist-development paradigm', in R.A. Dorfman (ed.), *Paradigms of Clinical Social Work*. New York: Brunner/Mazel.

Rosen, G.M., Lohr, J.M., McNally, R.J. and Herbert, J.D. (1998) 'Power therapies, miraculous claims, and the cures that fail', *Behavioural and Cognitive Psychotherapy*, 26: 99–101.

Roth, A. and Fonagy, P. (1996) *What Works for Whom? A Critical Review of Psychotherapy Research*. New York: Guilford Press.

Roy, A. (1982) 'Risk factors for suicide in psychiatric patients', *Archives of General Psychiatry*, 39: 1089–95.

Roy, A. (1992) 'Marked reductions in indexes of dopamine metabolism among patients with depression who attempted suicide', *Archives of General Psychiatry*, 49: 447–50.

Ruddell, P. (1997) 'General assessment issues', in S. Palmer and G. McMahon (eds), *Client Assessment*. London: Sage.

Ruddell, P. and Curwen, B. (1997) 'What type of help?', in S. Palmer and G. McMahon (eds), *Client Assessment*. London: Sage.

Rumelhart, D.E. (1981) 'Understanding understanding'. Tech Rep. CHIP 100) La Lolla, CA: University of California, San Diego, Center for Human Information Processing (January).

Rumelhart D.E. and Ortony, A. (1977) 'The representation of knowledge in memory', in R.C. Anderson, R.J. Spiro and W.E. Montague (eds), *Schooling and the Acquisition of Knowledge*. Hillsdale, NJ: Erlbaum.

Sachs, J.S. (1983) 'Negative factors in brief psychotherapy: an implicit assessment', *Journal of Consulting and Clinical Psychology*, 55: 557–64.

Safran, J.D. and Segal, Z.M. (1990a) *Interpersonal Process in Cognitive Therapy*. New York: Basic Books, Appendix II.

Safran, J.D. and Segal, Z.M. (1990b) *Interpersonal Process in Cognitive Therapy*. New York: Basic Books, Appendix I.

Salkovskis, P.M. (1985) 'Obsessional-compulsive problems: a cognitive-behavioural analysis', *Behavioural Research and Therapy*, 25: 571–83.

Salkovskis, P.M. (1988) 'Phenomenology, assessment and cognitive model of panic', in S. Rachman and J. Maser (eds), *Panic: Psychological Perspectives*. Hillsdale, NJ: Erlbaum.

Salkovskis, P.M. and Clark, D.M. (1991) 'Cognitive therapy for panic disorder', *Journal of Cognitive Psychotherapy*, 5: 215–26.

Salkovskis, P.M. and Kirk, J. (1989) 'Obsessional disorders', in K. Hawton, P. Salkovskis, J. Kirk and D. Clarke (eds), *Cognitive-Behavioural Therapy for Psychiatric Problems: A Practical Guide*. Oxford: Oxford University Press.

Salkovskis, P.M. and Warwick, H.M.C. (1985) 'Cognitive therapy of obsessive-compulsive disorder – treating treatment failures', *Behavioural Psychotherapy*, 13: 243–55.

Salkovskis, P.M., Jones, D.R.O. and Clark, D.M. (1986) 'Respiratory control in the treatment of panic attacks: replication and extension with concurrent measurement of behaviour and pCO_2', *British Journal of Psychiatry*, 148: 526–32.

Salkovskis, P.M. and Westbrook, D. (1987) 'Obsessive-compulsive disorder: clinical strategies for improving behavioural treatments', in H.R. Dent (ed.), *Clinical Psychology: Research and Development*. London: Croom Helm, pp. 200–13.

Salkovskis, P.M., Clark, D.M. and Hackman, A. (1991) 'Treatment of panic attacks using cognitive therapy without exposure or breathing training', *Behaviour Research and Therapy*, 29: 161–6.

Salkovskis, P.M., Forrester, E., Richards, H.C. and Morrison, R. (1998) 'The devil is in the detail: Conceptualising and treating obsessional problems', in W. Tarrier, A. Wells and G. Haddock (eds), *Treating Comples Cases: The Cognitive Behavioural Therapy Approach*. Chichester: John Wiley & Sons.

Schneidman, E. (1985) *Definition of Suicide*. New York: Wiley.

Scott, J. (1992) 'Cognitive behavioural therapy in primary care', in D.P. Gray, A. Wright, I. Pullin and G. Wilkinson (eds), *Psychiatry in General Practice*. London: Gaskill.

Scott, J. (1998) 'Where there's a will . . . cognitive therapy for people with chronic depressive disorders', in N. Tarrier, A. Wells and G. Haddock (eds), *Treating Comples Cases: The Cognitive Behavioural Therapy Approach*. Chichester: John Wiley & Sons.

Scott, M.J. and Palmer, S. (eds) (2000) *Trauma and Post-traumatic Stress Disorder*. London: Cassell.

Scott, M.J. and Stradling, S.G. (1992) *Counselling for Post-Traumatic Stress Disorder*. London: Sage.

Scott, M.J. and Stradling, S.G. (1998) *Brief Group Counselling: Integrating Individual and Group Cognitive-Behavioural Approaches*. Chichester: Wiley.

Scott, C., Scott, J., Tacchi, M.J. and Jones, R.H. (1994) 'Abbreviated cognitive therapy for depression: a pilot study in primary care', *Behavioural and Cognitive Psychotherapy*, 22: 57–64.

Shapiro, F. (1989) 'Eye movement desensitization: a new treatment for post-traumatic stress disorder', *Journal of Behavior Therapy and Experimental Psychiatry*, 20: 211–17.

Shapiro, F. (1995) *Eye Movement Desensitization and Reprocessing: Basic Principles, Protocols and Procedures*. New York: Guilford Press.

Skene, R.A. (1973) 'Construct shift in the treatment of a case of homosexuality', *British Journal of Medical Psychology*, 46: 287–92.

Skinner, B.F. (1953) *Science and Human Behavior*. New York: Free Press.

Smith, M.L., Glass, G.V. and Miller, T.I. (1980) *The Benefits of Psychotherapy*. Baltimore: Johns Hopkins University Press.

Spiegel, D. (1983) 'Hypnosis with psychotic patients', *American Journal of Clinical Hypnosis*, 10: 33–8.

Spivack, G., Platt, J.J. and Shure, M.B. (1976) *The Problem-Solving Approach to Adjustment*. San Francisco: Jossey Bass.

Strupp, H.H. (1986) 'Psychotherapy. Research, practice and public policy (how to avoid dead ends)', *American Psychologist*, 41: 120–30.

Suinn, R. and Richardson, F. (1971) 'Anxiety management training: a nonspecific behavior therapy program for anxiety control', *Behavior Therapy*, 2: 498–510.

Symonds, R.L. (1985) 'Psychiatric aspects of railway fatalities', *Psychological Medicine*, 15: 609–21.

Talmon, M. (1990) *Single Session Therapy: Maximising the Effect of the First (and Often Only) Therapeutic Encounter*. San Francisco, CA: Jossey Bass.

Teasdale, J.D., Fennel, M.J.V., Hibbert, G.A. and Amies, P.L. (1984) 'Cognitive therapy for major depressive disorder in primary care', *British Journal of Psychiatry*, 144: 400–6.

Thase, M.E., Bowler, K. and Harden, T. (1991) 'Cognitive behavior therapy of endogenous depression: part 2. Preliminary findings in 16 unmedicated inpatients', *Behavior Therapy*, 22: 469–77.

Trower, P., Casey, A. and Dryden, W. (1988) *Cognitive Behavioural Counselling in Action*. London: Sage.

Truax, C.B. and Carkhuff, R.R. (1967) *Towards Effective Counselling and Psychotherapy: Training and Practice*. Chicago: Aldine.

Vaillant, G. (1977) *Adaptation to Life*. Boston: Little Brown.

Wanigaratne, S. and Barker, C. (1995) 'Clients' preferences for styles of therapy', *British Journal of Clinical Psychology*, 34: 215–22.

Wasik, B. (1984) 'Teaching parents effective problem-solving: a handbook for professionals'. Unpublished manuscript. Chaple Hill: University Of North Carolina.

Weishaar, M.E. and Beck, A.T. (1992) 'Hopelessness and suicide', *International Review of Psychiatry*, 4: 177–84.

Weissman, A. (1979) 'The dysfunctional attitude scale: a validation study', *Dissertation Abstracts International*, 40: 1389–90B (University Microfilm no. 79-19,533).

Weissman, A. (1980) 'Assessing depressogenic attitudes: a validation study'. Paper presented at the 51st Annual Meeting of the Eastern Psychological Asociation, Hartford, Connecticut.

Weissman, A. and Beck, A.T. (1978) 'Development and validation of the dysfunctional attitude scale'. Paper presented at meeting of the Association for the Advancement of Behavior Therapy, Chicago, November.

Wells, A. (1995) 'Meta-cognitions and worry: a cognitive model of generalised anxiety disorder', *Behavioural and Cognitive Psychotherapy*, 23: 301–20.

Wells, A. (1997) *Cognitive Therapy of Anxiety Disorders: A Practice Manual and Conceptual Guide*. Chichester: John Wiley & Sons.

Wells, A. (1998) 'Cognitive Therapy of Social Phobia', in N. Tarrier, A. Wells and G. Haddock (eds), *Treating Comples Cases: The Cognitive Behavioural Therapy Approach*. Chichester: John Wiley & Sons.

Wessely, S., Rose, S. and Bisson, J. (1997) 'Brief psychological interventions (debriefing) for treating trauma-related symptoms and preventing post-traumatic stress disorder (Cochrane review)', in *The Cochrane Library*, 1, 1999. Oxford: Update Software.

Wolpe, J. and Lazarus, A.A. (1966) *Behavior Therapy Techniques*. New York: Pergamon.

Woody, G.E., Luborsky, L., McClellan, A.T., O'Brien, C.P., Beck, A.T., Blaine, J., Herman, I. and Hole, A. (1983) 'Psychotherapy for opiate addicts: does it work?', *Archives of General Psychiatry*, 40: 1081–6.

World Health Organisation (1992) *International Classification of Diseases*, 10th edn. Geneva: WHO.

Young, J.E. (1990) *Cognitive Therapy for Personality Disorders: A Schema-focussed Approach*. Sarasota, FL: Professional Resource Exchange.

Young, J.E. (1992) *Schema Conceptualisation Form*. New York: Cognitive Therapy Center of New York.

Zetzel, E. (1968) *The Capacity of Emotional Growth*. New York: International Universities Press.

Appendix 1

Questions to help examine unhelpful thinking

- Is it logical?
- Would a scientist agree with my logic?
- Where is the evidence for my belief?
- Where is the belief written (apart from inside my own head!)?
- Is my belief realistic?
- Would my friends and colleagues agree with my idea?
- Does everybody share my attitude? If not, why not?
- Am I expecting myself or others to be perfect as opposed to fallible human beings?
- What makes the situation so terrible, awful or horrible?
- Am I making a mountain out of a molehill?
- Will it seem this bad in one, three, six or twelve months' time?
- Will it be important for me in two years' time?
- Am I exaggerating the importance of this problem?
- Am I fortune telling with little evidence that the worse case scenario will actually happen?
- If I 'can't stand it' or 'can't bear it' what will really happen?
- If I 'can't stand it' will I really fall apart?
- Am I concentrating on my own (or others') weaknesses and neglecting strengths?
- Am I agonizing about how I think things should be instead of dealing with them as they are?
- Where is this thought or attitude getting me?
- Is my belief helping me to attain my goals?
- Is my belief goal focused and problem solving?
- If a friend made a similar mistake, would I be so critical?
- Am I thinking in all-or-nothing terms: is there any middle ground?
- Am I *labelling* myself, somebody or something else? Is this logical and a fair thing to do?
- Just because a problem has occurred does it mean that I/they/it are 'stupid', 'a failure', 'useless' or 'hopeless'?
- Am I placing rules on myself or others (e.g. shoulds or musts, etc.)? If so, are they proving helpful and constructive?

- Am I taking things too personally?
- Am I blaming others unfairly just to make myself (temporarily) feel better?

Appendix 2

Automatic thought form

What happened? This might be an event, thought, image or memory you had

What thought or thoughts went through you mind? Rate how much you believe each thought.	What emotions did you feel? How strong was each?
(a) .... %	(a) .... %
(b) .... %	(b) .... %
(c) .... %	(c) .... %
(d) .... %	(d) .... %

Tick the thinking errors for each thought   a   b   c   d
All-or-nothing thinking ....
Personalization/blame ....
Catastrophizing ....
Emotional reasoning ....
'Should' or 'must' statements ....
Mental filter ....
Discounting the positive ....
Overgeneralization ....
Magnification/minimization ....
Labelling ....
Jumping to conclusions – mind reading ....
Fortune telling ....

Alternative view for each thought	Rate			Rate
(a)	%	(b)		%
(c)	%	(d)		%

Rate emotions now				
(a)	%	(b)		%
(c)	%	(d)		%

Appendix 3

Cognitive conceptualization chart

Personal Development   **Cognitive Development**

Predisposing factors (early experience)

Precipitating factors (critical incident)   *Intermediate and core beliefs activated*

Maintaining factors (current situation)   *Negative automatic thoughts*

Emotions:

Behaviour:

Physiology:

Appendix 4

Belief change chart (BCC)

Old belief (unhelpful) ....

.... rate 0–100%

New belief (helpful) ....

.... rate 0–100%

Evidence for new belief rate 0–100%	Evidence for old belief rate 0–100%	Counter to old belief rate 0–100%
(Specific)	(Specific)	(Specific)

General helpful summary:

Appendix 5

Problem-solving worksheet

| 1 Problem I wish to resolve. | → | 2 What do I want? |

3 Brainstorm possible solutions

A
B
C
D

4 Desirable options

PROS	CONS
A (i) (ii) (iii) (iv)	(i) (ii) (iii) (iv)
B (i) (ii) (iii) (iv)	(i) (ii) (iii) (iv)
C (i) (ii) (iii) (iv)	(i) (ii) (iii) (iv)
D (i) (ii) (iii)	(i) (ii) (iii) (iv)

5 Decide on best solution(s)

6 What action will I take?

7 What happened?

Appendix 6

Preparing for setbacks

Use this form to identify possible setbacks before they occur and to work through what you can do in these situations.

Possible setbacks	My unhelpful response	What I can do – helpful response
Within first month		
Within three months		
Within six months		
Within one year		

Checklist of some things you can do

Go through therapy notebook – find similar situation and what you found helpful. Select three most helpful things in notebook/therapy and apply them to this situation. Use cognitive conceptualization; automatic thought form; problem-solving worksheet; belief change chart; step back from the situation; use relaxation; phone good friend; make fresh appointment; consider how terrible the event will be in six months' time.

Appendix 7

Handout form 1

Unhelpful belief: ....
....
....

<table>
<tr><td align="center">Advantages</td><td align="center">Disadvantages</td></tr>
</table>

Source: Adapted from Palmer and Burton (1996).

Appendix 8

Handout form 2

Helpful belief: ....

....

....

Advantages   Disadvantages

Source: Adapted from Palmer and Burton (1996).

Appendix 9

Handout form 3

Current behaviour: ....
....
....

Advantages	Disadvantages

Appendix 10

Handout form 4

Desired behaviour: ....
....
....

Advantages	Disadvantages

Appendix 11

Relaxation diary

Date	Session		Time in minutes	Relaxation technique used	Tension levels		Name:			Comments
	Began	Ended			Relaxed – 0 Tense – 10		Feelings			
					Before	After	Before	During	After	

Instructions: Note the date, time, duration and type of relaxation exercise used. On a scale of 0–10, where 0 represents a relaxed state and 10 represents a tense state, write down scores before and after a training exercise. Monitor emotions and bodily feelings in the appropriate column. Record any variations to the technique used and any other comments.

Source: Palmer, 1993b

Appendix 12

Major categories of psychiatric disorder

Mood disorders

Major depressive disorder	One or more depressive episodes, that is two weeks of depressed mood and loss of interest.
Dysthymic disorder	Two years of predominantly depressed mood not continuous and depressed symptoms not as severe as above.
Depressive disorder not otherwise specified	Does not reach criteria for major depressive disorder, or others as above.
Bipolar I disorder	One or more manic or mixed episodes often with depressive episode(s).
Bipolar II disorder	One or more major depressive episodes with one or more hypomanic episode(s).
Cyclothymic disorder	Hypomanic symptoms for two years and numerous episodes of depressive symptoms.
Bipolar disorder not otherwise specified	Bipolar features not meeting criteria for any specific bipolar disorder.
Mood disorder due to general medical condition	Disturbance in mood directly physiologically linked to general medical condition.
Substance-induced mood disorder	Disturbance in mood directly physiologically linked to a drug of abuse; medication or toxin exposure.
Mood disorder not otherwise specified	Mood symptoms not a specified mood disorder, depressive disorder or bipolar disorder.

Anxiety disorders

Panic attack	Sudden intense fear, apprehension; fearfulness and terror. During attack: shortness of breath; palpitations; chest pain and choking sensation; fear of losing control.

Agoraphobia	Avoidance of situations or places.
Panic disorder without agoraphobia	Recurrent panic attacks with persistent concern.
Panic disorder with agoraphobia	Recurrent panic attacks and agoraphobia.
Agoraphobia without history of panic attacks	Agoraphobia; panic-like symptoms, no real unexpected panic attacks
Specific phobia	Anxiety; feared object/situation avoidance behaviour.
Social phobia	Anxiety with social performance; avoidance behaviour.
Obsessive compulsive disorder	Obsessions and/or compulsions.
Post-traumatic stress disorder (PTSD)	Re-experiencing of traumatic event; increased arousal; avoidance of reminders of trauma; diagnosis after one month.
Acute stress disorder	Occurring immediately following extreme traumatic event.
Generalized anxiety disorder	Six months of panic and worry.
Anxiety disorder due to a general medical condition	Anxiety symptoms physiological consequence of general medical condition.
Substance-induced anxiety disorder	Anxiety symptoms physiological consequence of a drug of abuse; medication or toxin exposure.
Anxiety disorder not otherwise specified	Anxiety or phobic avoidance where the criteria do not meet the above.

Personality disorders

Paranoid personality disorder	Distrust, suspiciousness.
Schizoid personality disorder	Social detachment, restricted emotional expression.
Schizotypal personality disorder	Discomfort of close relationships, behavioural eccentricities, perceptual distortions.
Antisocial personality disorder	Disregard, violation of others' rights.
Borderline personality disorder	Impulsive, instability in interpersonal relationships.

Histrionic personality disorder	Lively, dramatic, attention seeking, emotional excitability.
Narcissistic personality disorder	Grandiose sense of self-importance, lacks empathy, needs admiration.
Avoidant personality disorder	Social inhibition, feelings of inadequacy, hypersensitivity.
Dependent personality disorder	Submissive, clinging.
Obsessive personality disorder	Orderliness, perfectionism, control.
Personality disorder not otherwise specified	Traits for personality disorder but none specific.

Eating disorders

| Anorexia nervosa | Refusal to maintain minimum body weight, refusal of food, distorted perception of shape, size or body. Afraid of weight gain, amenorrhoea (absence of menstruation). |
| Bulimia nervosa | Binge eating, self-induced vomiting, misuse of laxatives, diuretics, fasting, excessive exercise. |

Schizophrenia/psychotic disorders

Schizophrenia	Delusions or hallucinations, disorganized speech, disorganized behaviour, catatonic behaviour.
Schizophreniform	Symptoms equivalent to schizophrenia disturbance, one to six months' decline in functioning.
Schizoaffective disorder	Disturbance of mood, delusions, hallucinations.
Delusional disorder	Non-bizarre delusions.
Brief psychotic disorder	Psychotic disturbance lasting more than a day, less than one month.
Shared psychotic disorder	Influenced by another who already has a delusion.
Psychotic disorder due to general medical condition	Psychotic symptoms physiologically linked to general medical condition.
Substance-induced psychotic disorder	Physiologically linked to drug abuse, medication or toxin exposure.

Sleep disorders

Primary sleep disorders	Dyssomnias: difficulty initiating sleep or maintaining sleep, narcolepsy, breathing-related sleep disorders.
	Parasomnias: abnormal behaviour or physiological events, such as nightmares, sleep walking.
Sleep disorder related to another mental disorder	Related to mental disorder, such as mood or anxiety.
Sleep disorder related to general medical condition	Direct physiological effects.
Substance-induced sleep disorder	Disturbance in sleep severe, direct effect of a drug of abuse, medication, toxin.

Index